Experiential Activities for Intercultural Learning

Experiential Activities for Intercultural Learning

H. Ned Seelye
editor

INTERCULTURAL PRESS
A Nicholas Brealey Publishing Company

BOSTON • LONDON

First published by Intercultural Press, a Nicholas Brealey Publishing Company, in 1996. For information, contact:

Intercultural Press, Inc.,
a division of
Nicholas Brealey Publishing
100 City Hall Plaza, Suite 501
Boston, MA 02108, USA
Tel: (+) 617-523-3801
Fax: (+) 617-523-3708
www.interculturalpress.com

Nicholas Brealey Publishing
3-5 Spafield St., Clerkenwell
London, EC1R 4QB, UK
Tel: 44-207-239-0360
Fax: 44-207-239-0370
www.nbrealey-books.com

ISBN-13: 978-1-877864-33-9
ISBN-10: 1-877864-33-1

Printed in the United States of America

10   09   08   07   06   8   9   10   11 12

Library of Congress Cataloging-in-Publication Data
Experiential Activities for Intercultural Learning / H. Ned Seelye, editor.
p. cm.
Includes bibliographical references.
ISBN 1-877864-33-1
1. Multicultural education—United States—Activity programs. 2. Interpersonal communication—United States. I. Seelye, H. Ned
LC1099.3.E97 1996
370.19'6—dc20   95-36960
CIP

Table of Contents

Section III: Courting the Intercultural Perspective

Section IV: Working Together

Introduction

H. Ned Seelye

The Antecedents

Intercultural communication has piqued the interest of trainers, teachers, and scholars in a number of disciplines for some time, although this focus has always been peripheral to the central concerns of their respective academic guilds. More likely than not, they labored in ignorance of what their colleagues in other disciplines and in other organizations were doing to enhance the intercultural skills of students or workshop participants.

One early effort to exchange information was made by David S. Hoopes and Toby S. Frank under the aegis of the Intercultural Communications Network. The Network gathered and informally distributed cross-cultural training materials, intercultural communication course syllabi, and other writings through a now out-of-print series, Readings in Intercultural Communication. Teachers and trainers were asked what objectives they were pursuing, how they organized their training, and what resources they used. The Network also published *Intercultural Sourcebook*, a more systematic survey of cross-cultural training techniques and methodologies, which was another useful vehicle for sharing ideas. This, too, was out-of-print, and Volume I of what will be a two-volume set has recently been reissued, in an extensively revised and expanded edition, by the Intercultural Press, edited by Sandra M. Fowler and Monica Mumford.

The formation of a common meeting place for these colleagues occurred in 1975 with the birth of SIETAR, the Society for Intercultural Education, Training and Research (which later became SIETAR International). The first SIETAR conference twenty-one years ago was fascinating in its human dynamics. Many professionals discovered they weren't the only peacock on the lawn, that other colleagues had pretensions of deep (and somewhat exclusive) expertise in things cross-cultural, and that the ideas of their colleagues often sharply differed from their own. This did not necessarily brighten their day. In one large conference session, an American psychologist rose from the floor to talk about ego strength, only to have his own tested by a participant from India who immediately rebutted the American by saying that in many Eastern societies there is no "I" apart from the rest of the universe of people and things. And so it went for several contentious but enormously stimulating days. Ruffled feathers were smoothed by the prevailing eagerness to learn; subsequent meetings have been characterized by an easy acceptance of others and an interest in novel ideas.

Practical-minded trainers and teachers sometimes fidget during long discussions of the many (more than twenty to date) theoretical constructs underpinning cross-cultural training. (An excellent source for many of these discussions is the *International Journal of Intercultural Relations*.) "Give me something practical to use next week," teachers and trainers pleaded.

Early attempts to respond to this call resulted in *Guidelines for Peace Corps Cross-Cultural Training* (1970); *A Manual of Teaching Techniques for Intercultural Education* (1971); and the first book to suggest a specific cross-cultural learning methodology, along with illustrative activities for foreign language teachers, *Teaching Culture* (1974; its revised editions are aimed at intercultural teachers and trainers from any field). Three colleagues provided teachers and trainers, in 1977, with *A Manual of Structured Experiences for Cross-Cultural Learning*. They modeled the general format of their book on a series published by University Associates (now Pfeiffer & Company) for organizational development and human relations trainers.

The Current Volume

This volume, the first in a projected series, provides teachers and trainers on the front lines with a provocative essay that discusses both theory and practice, followed by thirty-two practical activities to engender understanding and skill in one facet or another of intercultural contact. Just being practical, of course, is not enough. The activities selected for this series also are purposeful and economic. That is, they are aimed at parsimoniously advancing a cross-culturally relevant objective.

We try to give parental credit to the creators of the activities included in this series, but the genesis of many training activities is hard to pin down. Many activities are anonymously authored, others are borrowed or "retold" by trainers who fail to footnote the prior authorship, and most of the activities are edited by hundreds of practitioners (who may feel the activity is now theirs). Everyone who uses an activity tends to salt it liberally to his or her own taste. Many of the activities' "originators" are not so much parents as godparents. The editor of this series has himself further edited many of the activities selected for this volume; you, reader, are invited to continue the evolutionary process.

Current Strengths and Weaknesses

The up side of the current state of the art regarding intercultural training activities is that there have evolved over the last twenty or thirty years—and are available in books—hundreds (but not thousands) of mostly discrete experiential learning activities. Most of these have been designed and used by American trainers and teachers who face largely American trainees; generally they aim at short-term adjustment to a country the trainees have not visited. Most of these activities are designed to allow adolescent and adult learners to discover that there are special skills needed to communicate across cultural boundaries. A few even go beyond awakening awareness to developing some handy skills. A few of the activities are simulations that allow the participant to experience a measure of what it feels like to be in an intercultural situation. The vast majority of the activities focus on understanding that is culturally general in nature. No matter where a participant is headed, geographically speaking, he or she profits from greater awareness of the principles governing accurate communication, rapport, and persuasion in foreign settings.

The very strengths of the current state of the art suggest areas in which teachers and trainers might invest future creative energies.

- A closer analysis of which culturally general knowledge and skills are needed to survive both short- *and* long-term sojourns would aid designers of intercultural learning activities to both sharpen and broaden their coverage.

- Identification of the skills needed by trainees will be honed by taking into account the extent to which role and gender considerations affect the behavior required to get along in a novel cultural setting.

- Theory with implications for intercultural communication is generated by a number of disciplines. Many of the current applications to the intercultural field have been enriched by theory from the fields of psychology and organizational development; some come from anthropology and sociology. Where are the learning activities based on social science models from linguistics, economics, history, and political science, and models from the sciences such as sociobiology and human genetics? Perhaps models useful for understanding the ebb and flow, the warp and woof of intercultural communication will emerge from physics, as investigators seek patterns in events that until recently have been considered random (e.g., chaos theory). The field of pedagogy, one would suspect, would be a promising source of learning models. Where are the activities based on non–Western philosophies? Do Tao and Zen suggest any apt intercultural-learner activities?

- Activities that feature the role of *language* (and not just English) in communicating with host nationals are now largely ignored by the extant intercultural activities. Would activities along these lines be helpful?

- Current learning objectives too often are pie-in-the-sky, macro goals, rather than distinct and succinct, narrowly focused learning objectives (preferably student-centered) that contribute a strategic building block rather than attempt the whole edifice at once in a 40-minute exercise.

- Most of the current learning activities are built around one or more incidents of cross-cultural misunderstanding. This "critical-incident" approach (whether in role-playing skits, case studies, simulations, or whatever vehicle), involving as it does the participant in actively finding the cause of the misunderstanding, has been demonstrated by social psychologists (e.g., Harry Triandis) to offer advantages over traditional approaches such as reading a book about the culture. More research into the short-term *and* long-term effectiveness of various training approaches in meeting their objectives could be a big help to practitioners who currently have to rely on participants' immediate satisfaction with the training for evaluative feedback.

- Adjusting to life in a specific place requires skill in a number of idiosyncratic behaviors. Where are the culturally specific training activities?

- Where are the activities to reduce domestic interethnic, interracial, religious, class, and gender conflict, activities that take cognizance of the particular history and psychosocial dynamics of the targeted groups?

- Do we have enough activities for people with varying learning styles? The "comfortable" (i.e., traditional) learning style in most of the world is a deductive, pre-Deweyan, lecture-rote-memorization approach. When trainers or teachers face learners *in* other cultural settings, or *from* other cultural settings, is there a need to modify how we present experiential activities? Do the activities themselves need revision? Do we need more activities that focus on the processing of visual images or nonverbal communication? It may be worth noting that part of the popularity of adult experiential activities in the United States is that they contrast refreshingly with the more formal presentations of knowledge and skills that we all experienced (with varying degrees of success) in secondary school and college.

- Most children engage in intercultural communication, if not in their neighborhoods, then at school. They also accompany their parents on multinational sojourns. Besides the University of Denver's Center for Teaching International Relations, who is developing training activities for preadolescents?

- Most current intercultural activities are highly derivative. We need more innovative activities. (In this regard, it is a sign of professionalism to acknowledge authors of prior activities that may have stimulated the creation of the present version of their experiential learning activity.)

Our toolbox of intercultural learning activities may not yet be full.

Call for Learning Activities and Format Considerations

Submissions for future volumes are welcomed and should be addressed to the Intercultural Press. They should follow the general format of the current volume. We are especially looking for activities that focus on building intercultural skills and that are new and based on up-to-date theory (no more variations on R. Garry Shirts's wonderfully successful *BaFá BaFá* [Simile II, 1973], please), and for activities that are fun to do. Activities developed by trainers in and for non-Western societies will be looked upon with special grace and gratitude as will those dealing with multicultural and diversity issues in any country.

The format in which the learning units are cast contributes to their usefulness, and we will appreciate user feedback. The units need to be brief while avoiding being cryptic. They need to spell out the linear steps involved. This Betty Crocker approach revolutionized cooking and we think the intercultural learning tools this approach provides can be useful to teachers and trainers, too. This takes nothing away from the artistry of teaching. Sheila Ramsey's essay that precedes this volume's learning activities forcefully highlights the pivotal role of the inspired teacher-trainer.

The current link between theory and practice is a bit shaky. More often than not, theory, if mentioned at all, is described incompletely and cryptically. (Succinct is in, cryptic is out.) For example, there are many theories of ethnocentrism (see LeVine and Campbell 1972), yet activities to reduce ethnocentrism seldom seem to be tied to any one identifiable theory. A paragraph that provides the theoretical setting and rationale for the author's learning unit enhances the presentation.

There is a continuous need to identify and update resources that practitioners may find useful. These resources include both basic theory and other sources of practical training units with compatible objectives. Complete bibliographical data is necessary (future submitters please take note). The reader should not have to go to the library to identify references properly. The author of the activity provides that service.

Virtually all learning units need a follow-up or debriefing section at the end. It is very helpful when this procedure is carefully considered and spelled out in detail.

Trainer tips are helpful, a brief note by the designer of the activity sharing information he or she gained in using the activity with flesh-and-blood people.

Finally, the activity's usefulness is greatly enhanced when any instructional materials needed to do the activity are provided as handouts.

In this volume, we have tried to move closer to our realizable goal of bringing good intercultural learning activities to trainers and teachers. We are excited by the activities selected for inclusion in this volume. A lot of interesting stuff is going on out there. Sometimes the skills it takes to create an exciting, purposeful activity that blooms in the trainee's mind and heart and, at the same time, has sharp objectives and stated theoretical implications or limitations, do not comfortably coexist in the same curriculum developer. Maybe a little collaboration between engagingly charismatic and creative teacher-trainers and those who are less demonstrative, more scholarly-oriented, research-minded types, can spark synergy.

David S. Hoopes, editor-in-chief of Intercultural Press, and Toby S. Frank, president of Intercultural Press, provided invaluable assistance in getting this volume ready for press.

References Cited

Fowler, Sandra M, and Monica G. Mumford, eds. *Intercultural Sourcebook: Cross-Cultural Training Methods,* vol. 1. Yarmouth, ME: Intercultural Press, 1995.

Holmes, Henry, and Stephen Guild, eds. *A Manual of Teaching Techniques for Intercultural Education.* Prepared for UNESCO, University of Massachusetts: Center for International Education, October 1971. Out of print.

Hoopes, David S., ed. Readings in Intercultural Communication, vols. 1-5. Pittsburgh: Intercultural Communications Network, 1974-1977. Out of print.

International Journal of Intercultural Relations. Elmsford, NY: Pergamon Press.

LeVine, Robert A., and Donald T. Campbell. *Ethnocentrism: Theories of Conflict, Ethnic Attitudes and Group Behavior.* New York: Wiley, 1972.

Seelye, H. Ned. *Teaching Culture: Strategies for Intercultural Communication.* Lincolnwood, IL: National Textbook, 3d ed., 1993.

———. *Teaching Culture: Techniques for Foreign Language Educators.* Skokie, IL: National Textbook, 1974. Out of print.

Weeks, William H., Paul B. Pedersen, and Richard W. Brislin, eds. *A Manual of Structured Experiences for Cross-Cultural Learning.* Pittsburgh: SIETAR, University of Pittsburgh, 1977. Rev. ed., Yarmouth, ME: Intercultural Press, in press [1996].

Wight, Albert R., and Mary Anne Hammons, eds. *Guidelines for Peace Corps Cross-Cultural Training.* Published for the Peace Corps Office of Training Support, Washington, DC. Estes Park, CO: Center for Research and Education, March 1970. Out of print.

Creating a Context: Methodologies in Intercultural Teaching and Training

Sheila Ramsey

Introduction

> In today's highly interdependent world, individuals and nations can no longer resolve many of their problems by themselves. We need one another.
>
> —The 14th Dalai Lama of Tibet

As a formalized field of study, intercultural communication is barely twenty-five years old. The organization representing this field, the International Society for Intercultural Education, Training and Research, celebrated its twentieth anniversary in 1994. Twenty-five years ago it was rare to find an intercultural communication course taught at the university level. Today university students select among intercultural programs and institutes; the choices are broad, varied, and of high quality. Clients in corporations, health care, or government who seek consultation or training in intercultural matters are also faced with the opportunity for choice.

This rapid proliferation of variety and sophistication in the field asks us to reconsider the unique theoretical perspectives at its core. Such reflection upon essentials of effective intercultural interaction is not simply "nice," it is critical in determining what this field has to offer as we approach a new milennium.

In this volume containing methods for intercultural work, we first reexamine the very *decisions* we make about methodologies. This process of looking anew can bring greater consciousness to our decisions, so that both our creation and our use of methodologies best serve the intercultural learning we wish to facilitate.

To begin, what is meant by "methodology"? In this context, it is an intentionally constructed, time-bounded event meant to provide an opportunity for intercultural learning. In the development of intercultural communication as a discipline, several common methodological forms have emerged for teaching and training. These include the *case study*, the *critical incident*, the *culture assimilator*, the *role play*, and the *simulation*. In addition, as this collection illustrates, many highly innovative, free-form activities and exercises focus learning around specific objectives for specific audiences.

Today, there are hundreds of learning activities expressly written for intercultural audiences, with thousands more adaptable for such use. These, then, are the tools of our trade. Yet we can sharpen the discernment which guides our decisions about whether to use a particular method as is, whether to modify it, or whether to create an entirely new method to fit particular situations.

Taking a Fresh Look

Years of effort and experience have brought us to this moment when our toolbox is relatively full. But we also know that perceptions have been subtly shifting about the role of "a method" in facilitating intercultural learning. It has become too easy to be mechanical, to believe that a certain method will produce predictable desired outcomes, and thus to see our role as one of picking and choosing. From such a perspective, it is easy to believe that the magic and life of a training program lie in the choice of just the right method for the learning objective and audience.

Methodologies do impart flavor and distinction. But there is no life in a method itself. The understandings and the very spirit that enter a training program, a classroom, or a consultation session do not lie in a direct line between objectives, method, and design. Learning is a dynamic, cocreative process which comes alive in the interaction of the leader with the participants. Such interaction occurs not only within the boundaries set by content, but by the overall purpose of the program as it aligns with specific learning objectives and methodology. A skilled leader remembers this alignment with a larger purpose and consciously selects and uses a methodology rather than being used by it.

Just as a leader works with participants, so one works with a chosen method: the place of cocreation and spontaneity is of utmost importance. One can be continually surprised by what is revealed even if the particular method has been used a thousand times. To the degree that we wish clients to integrate and apply their learning in daily life, we can remember that we are engaged in facilitating living events. Our methods are more inspiring and motivating as we acknowledge that, at its essence, our work is a creative act.[1] In this way, our methodologies are realigned to enlighten and enliven, rather than direct, our acts of creation.

To reexamine the decisions made about the methods we use, it is helpful to explore several areas. These include (1) some of the basic tenets of intercultural communication, which serve as filters through which we construct and implement our work, (2) selected aspects of the larger design process, and (3) our roles as professionals facilitating intercultural learning.

---

[1] I am especially indebted to graduate work I did, in 1974-1976, with Mary Lou Smith, of the Graduate School of Public and International Affairs, University of Pittsburgh. Her concept of "emergent design" continues to heavily influence my work.

The Shape of Our World

Let us begin with the well-known analogy of the iceberg. What is "under the water-line" is of more importance, as one seeks to adapt to an unfamiliar culture, than what can be seen upon first encounter. What then is under the waterline of the intercultural field itself? What is the metatheory or metaperspective from which the field of intercultural communication generates? What are the processes that are constant throughout the consulting, training, and education carried out in the name of intercultural communication?

Submerged Assumptions

Culture. The shape of our world grows out of the way the major actor, culture, is conceptualized. Culture is a frame of reference consisting of learned patterns of behavior, values, assumptions, and meaning, which are shared to varying degrees of interest, importance, and awareness with members of a group; culture is the story of reality that individuals and groups value and accept as a guide for organizing their lives.

This definition refers to what is called culture with a small *c*, not culture with a big *C*. The latter, objective culture, refers to the traditional view of culture as theater, dance, music, and art. Small *c* culture, subjective culture, has no existence except in human behavior. It has to do with how we create meaning in our lives and how we behave according to the meanings we create. Patterns of behavior and values are learned and passed through generations and across groups. They are widely shared and not frequently overtly discussed. Simultaneously they provoke emotional reactions when violated, are most obvious when in contrast, can be quite paradoxical, and may be both accepted and rejected at the same time.

Culture is an abstraction; it cannot actually be seen or touched. The analogy of the wind is helpful in grasping the abstract and secondhand nature of this concept. One cannot see the wind. So how do we know it is a windy day? We see a flag moving, we hear leaves of a tree rubbing against each other, we feel a pressure on our skin. The name we give the difference or the feeling is "wind." So too with culture. We see people acting in agreed-upon ways in the face of similar situations. We hear people using the same sounds in reference to common objects or experiences. We notice people moving their bodies in certain ways—making choices in their lives about where to live, what to eat, how to learn, how to work and love—in response to similar events and experiences, and we say "Oh, those people belong to the same culture."

We must remember that culture is an abstraction produced by thought. The effects of forgetting this are nicely illustrated by John C. Condon (1993) as he speaks about thirteen reasons to avoid the word "culture." He suggests that as culture becomes a thing, we begin to believe that "culture is a place or a place one comes from." We also can believe that "if I understand your culture, I will understand you." In the first case, culture is thought to be external to people. In the second case, a rigid definition of what a member of *X* culture must be like can be to the detriment of a person who identifies with X but is not at all like the popular image.[2] For example, in a workshop addressing methodologies, participants had just finished a movement exercise which allowed them to develop an in-depth intuitive sense of their partner from another national culture. In the discussion, a young woman asked, "I feel like I understand my partner in a way I didn't before, but what does it tell me about her culture?" The importance of getting to know her partner was less valuable than her search for greater understanding of an abstraction.

In studying culture we are studying the common rules, the common assumptions, the common values that are the foundations of the external behavior which we can see, touch, and feel. What function does this abstraction of culture have in our lives? We feel a sense of belonging, a sense of inclusion, for there are others like us. We have a frame of reference, a point of view, through which to look at and make sense of the world; we receive reinforcement for this way of looking at and being in the world. We have guidelines about how to translate our meanings into action. We look around and see that we are not crazy or mad in the choices we make; our lives are structurally coherent and make sense.

Intercultural Communication. What then of intercultural communication? The second major actor that gives shape to our world is the concept of communication. A most simple, elegant, and well-accepted definition arises from the work of the late Dean Barnlund. Communication is the creation of meaning. We as humans are meaning-making creatures. To quote Dr. Barnlund:

> It is impossible to exist without acting; impossible to act without interpreting…. The world is possibility, no more, no less. We are born into an environment so varied, so complex, so devoid of inherent meaning as to overwhelm the senses. Yet no matter how chaotic it seems, we must make it intelligible.[3]

Barnlund also suggests that any communicative act, the act of making meaning, is contextual, irreversible, and not repeatable; it does not depend upon anyone being intentional and, in actuality, we cannot *not* communicate!

Intercultural communication becomes the creation of shared meanings among people who are more different than they are alike. The communication scholar Young Yun Kim states this succinctly:

> The crux of intercultural communication that distinguishes it from the rest of the (communication) field is the relatively high degree of difference in the experiential backgrounds of the communicators due to cultural differences. An underlying assumption here is that individuals who belong to the same culture generally share greater commonality (or homogeneity) in their overall experiential backgrounds than those from different cultures.[4]

---

[2] John C. Condon, "Some Reasons to Avoid the Word 'Culture'," personal communication, Tokyo, Japan (December 1993).
[3] Dean Barnlund, "Toward an Ecology of Communication," in *Rigor and Imagination: Essays in the Legacy of Gregory Bateson*, edited by J. A. Weakland and C. Wilder (New York: Praeger, 1982), 74.
[4] Young Yun Kim, "Intercultural Communication Competence: A Systems-Theoretic View," in *Readings on Communicating with Strangers: An Approach to Intercultural Communication*, edited by W. B. Gudykunst and Y. Y. Kim (New York: McGraw-Hill, 1992), 371-78.

The Domain of Difference. In intercultural communication, not only is difference our domain, but it is our avenue into understanding. We make the assumption that we can best find our shared humanness by examining, allowing, and respecting differences. Indeed, in intercultural situations we know that people must be allowed to be different from each other. To the degree that a focus is placed on similarity, there is a good chance that the other can only be seen through comparison with and likeness to ourselves.

Evidence of the importance of this assumption can be seen in the distinctions made in our field between sympathy and empathy. We are sympathetic as we try to understand another by putting self in the unfamiliar shoes: "I know how you feel because I have been there too" is obviously based upon a process of projected similarity in trying to imagine how the other feels based upon one's own experience. So emerges the golden rule: "Do unto others as you would have them do unto you." Empathy, on the other hand, involves doing one's best to imagine another person's situation without projecting self into it. We try to enter into the others' experience more purely from their point of view. Thus emerges the silver rule: "Do unto others as they would have you do unto them." This suggests attention to listening and the capability to identify and monitor the habit of projection. Such definitions point to the assumption, shared widely in this field, that another person becomes fully human to the extent that we are able to let the other be different from ourselves.[5]

Interaction. In addition to being based on particular definitions of culture and communication and to building understanding through a valuing of difference, this field is characterized by attention to interaction among peoples who are more different than alike. Cross-cultural comparisons may supply part of the information necessary to support people who are learning to live and work in new situations. From the comparative perspective, intercultural communication is about identifying cultural differences of the *other* and comparing/contrasting such differences with *self*; for example, how do Japanese make decisions in a corporate setting? However, the heart of our work lies in the exploration of how people adapt and adjust when directly encountering others who practice unfamiliar processes of perceiving, valuing, and behaving in the world. From the interactive perspective, one learns how to participate in decision making *with* Japanese in corporate settings.

This certainly does involve the learning of a great deal of culturally specific information. In educational and consultative work, much time and attention are given to learning culturally specific knowledge and then applying such knowledge in contextually defined interactions with those who are from different backgrounds and experience. The focus on interacting with those who are culturally different is supported by research about predictors of effective intercultural performance and how to become competent in another culture.[6]

---

[5] Milton Bennett, "Overcoming the Golden Rule: Sympathy and Empathy," in *Communication Yearbook 3*, edited by D. Nimmo (Washington, DC: International Communication Association, 1979).

[6] Richard Wiseman and J. Koester, eds, *Intercultural Communication Competence* (Newbury Park: Sage, 1993).

At the Very Core. Accepting the wide variety of forms that intercultural work can take, it remains the case that our work, at its core, is directed toward only a few very fundamental themes. These are developing the abilities and capacities to

- live and work effectively with difference/unfamiliarity/ambiguity,
- live and work effectively with change,
- access creativity, and
- consciously manage one's state of being.

These themes are the focus of current research and serve as the foundation of several developmental models that give logic to the design of training and consultation efforts. For example, William Gudykunst posits forty-nine axioms describing the relationship between effective interpersonal and intergroup communication and the ability to manage uncertainty and its emotional equivalent, anxiety, when in unfamiliar situations. In a training program, participants would be encouraged to discover their personal thresholds above which there is so much apprehension that one wishes to avoid contact with another and below which one is not motivated to attempt communication. Such discovery and the self-management of interactions influenced by that knowledge base Gudykunst anchors in the concept of "mindfulness."[7]

All of these basic themes serve as a foundation for two developmental models which are rapidly becoming acknowledged as basic conceptual frameworks for designing intercultural training programs. In his "Developmental Model of Intercultural Sensitivity," Milton Bennett describes the stages through which a person's relationship to difference progresses. From denial one moves through acceptance into integration. The major shift from the ethnocentric stages to the ethnorelative stages occurs as one develops the ability for self-reflection and the realization that each person is the creator of the world she or he lives in.[8] Although addressing a different topic, William Perry's scheme of cognitive and ethical development also describes the unfolding of self-reflection and ways of living with difference and change. The journey moves from dualism, in which right and wrong are clearly marked, into contextual relativism, in which one evaluates any position by its appropriateness to a defined context, and then into "commitment in relativism." Here it is possible to accept the viability of many points of view but one makes personal choices which are grounded in a critical assessment of context. In this last stage, one becomes responsible for creating one's own ethical guidelines and making personal choices.[9]

---

[7] William Gudykunst, "Toward a Theory of Effective Interpersonal and Intergroup Communication: An Anxiety/Uncertainty Management (AUM) Perspective," in *Intercultural Communication Competence*, edited by Richard Wiseman and J. Koester (Newbury Park: Sage, 1993).

[8] Milton Bennett, "Toward Ethnorelativism: A Developmental Model of Intercultural Sensitivity," in *Education for the Intercultural Experience*, edited by R. Michael Paige (Yarmouth, ME: Intercultural Press, 1993), 25.

[9] William Perry, *Forms of Intellectual and Ethical Development in the College Years: A Scheme* (New York: Holt, 1970).

In becoming self-reflective and developing a heightened consciousness of self, the role of difference is crucial. A basic tenet of intercultural work is that it is through contrast that one has the opportunity to learn most about oneself; what better contrast experience can be had than to live and work intimately with others who do not share one's most basic assumptions and values? Kenneth Boulding tells us:

> The human nervous system is structured in such a way that the patterns that govern behavior and perception come into consciousness only when there is a deviation from the familiar. Intercultural encounters provide such situations of deviation from the familiar as individuals are faced with things that do not follow their hidden program.[10]

The growth of consciousness, through encountering difference, is fundamentally a process wherein the meaning of an event is available to a vast array of interpretations. The same experience can be labeled a stimulating and challenging opportunity or a painful and disorienting one which cannot be forgotten too soon. In encountering difference lies an opportunity for self-reflection and the development of self-knowledge. The opportunity exists and the choice is ours. Peter Adler comments about the choice available in the experience of culture shock:

> Culture shock is thought of as a profound learning experience that leads to a high degree of self awareness and personal growth. Rather than being a disease for which adaptation is the cure, culture shock is likewise at the very heart of a cross-cultural learning experience. It is an experience in self-understanding and change.[11]

Ultimately, the intercultural journey seems to be one of facing ourselves as we become aware of and responsible for the meanings we create and through which we then interpret our experiences. Whether or not we are successful in an intercultural encounter is directly related to the management of our own state of being. This is illustrated in the theory and research relating cultural experiences to identity development. Janet Bennett explains the concept of "constructive marginality" as it describes persons who operate

> ...outside all cultural frames of reference by virtue of their ability to consciously raise any assumption to a meta-level (level of self-reference). In other words, there is no natural cultural identity for a marginal person. There are no unquestioned assumptions, no intrinsically right behaviors...constructive marginality is the experience of one's self as a constant creator of one's own reality.[12]

---

[10] Kenneth Boulding as cited in *Readings on Communicating with Strangers*, edited by W. B. Gudykunst and Y. Y. Kim (New York: McGraw-Hill, 1992), 406.
[11] Peter Adler, "Culture Shock and the Cross-Cultural Learning Experience," in *Toward Internationalism*, edited by L. F. Luce and E. C. Smith (Cambridge: Newbury Press, 1987), 24–35.
[12] Janet Bennett, "Cultural Marginality: Identity Issues in Intercultural Training," in *Education for the Intercultural Experience*, edited by R. Michael Paige (Yarmouth, ME: Intercultural Press, 1993), 109–135.

The intercultural field is based upon the acceptance of difference, the exploration of interaction, the belief that we are meaning makers who construct and reconstruct our own realities. As such, the work that is carried out in the name of "intercultural training" is of a distinctive character.

In such work, we are leading and supporting people to explore new views of reality and to develop new frames of reference for categorizing and explaining behavior. We are suggesting that one can adjust to new ways of being and doing and that life will be richer and deeper for having encountered differences. We call attention to strategies for encountering change, unfamiliarity, and ambiguity in creative ways. Our work demonstrates that it is both possible and positive to realize that what is taken as "common sense" is indeed "cultural sense." It becomes possible to see that the consensual reality in which one lives is only real to the extent that one believes and accepts the power of that consensus. And we suggest that such realization is partner to the development of consciousness, that is, the capability to become self-reflective about habits of heart and mind and the ways these are expressed in daily life.

Yet it is not guaranteed that participation in intercultural interactions will bring people to know themselves, or anyone else, in any greater depth than before the interaction. There is no direct relationship between engaging in an intercultural experience and developing competence in dealing with ambiguous situations, coming to truly value the less familiar ways of others, or caring about life lived from a self-reflective point of view.

We who find ourselves in the role of leader, teacher, or coach of those who are encountering difference, work in a world of possibilities and opportunities. It could very well be that decisions about whether to step onto that path of profound learning that can lead to the self-awareness and personal growth spoken about by Adler and experiencing one's self as a constant creator of one's own reality are decisions begun in our presence. Fundamental choices are being made in our second-language or intercultural communication classrooms, our predeparture or re-entry workshops, our consultations about leadership and strategic planning, our counseling with home-stay families, or in our mediation to resolve international conflicts.

In this sense the fundamental role we play is that of one who enables and guides a journey of discovery which is given a special character by the intercultural nature of the interactions involved. Often we enable this journey by intentionally constructing events. When this is so, we face decisions about choosing and/or creating the methodologies within which we will guide the learning experience.

The Building Blocks

Any method is, of course, set within the larger frame of an entire workshop or course. There are decisions to be made about content and sequence and about how to place the method within the entire flow of the learning experience. One must carefully examine a particular method and make distinctions regarding applicability to the client or trainee, the logistical match with the situation, the possible impact upon and support for learning objectives, and the degree of comfort and freedom which the facilitator may feel in using the method. How are such distinctions to be made? One answer to such a question is: practice, practice, practice! However, there are road marks that can provide clarity along the way. Consider the workshops and seminars you have conducted; think of a time when you used some methodology and were gratified with the interaction and learning that ensued. Then think of just the opposite experience. What were the factors which contributed to these different outcomes? This question has been asked at the beginning of a number of workshops exploring methodologies used in intercultural work.[13]

Factors Contributing to Effective Use of Methodologies

Application to "real life" was clear

Relationship to audience's need was clear

Goals and purposes were clear

Participants became involved

Learning was personalized

Affective domain was important

Participants became aware of their own values

Participants were used as resources

Learning was cooperative; people taught each other

Sessions alternated between theory and experience

Facilitator was well prepared and comfortable with the method used

Facilitator knew the audience and could establish rapport

Facilitator could shift style and change agenda relative to the learners' reactions

Facilitator could model the learning points

Facilitator could "metaprocess," i.e., reflect upon the training process being used and upon the current situation in the workshop

Atmosphere was one of self-discovery and continuous revelation

Experience was fun

Factors Contributing to Ineffective Use of Methodologies

Program was a "package"; participants' needs were not assessed

Methods chosen did not fit the personalities and the politics of the audience

Tasks were too easy, not sufficiently challenging, and the participants lost interest

Poor pacing and use of time

Entire environment was not conducive to learning

Goals were in conflict with each other

Audience did not understand the exercise instructions

---

[13] "Methods in Intercultural Teaching and Training" workshops led by Sheila Ramsey and sponsored by Cross-Cultural Training Services, Tokyo, Japan; 1990-1992.

Participants could not see the significance of the experience

Participants' identities were threatened

Facilitator did not like the method and the participants could feel it

Facilitator was too attached to the outcome

Facilitator had preconceived ideas of what learning should occur

Facilitator focused too much on the material at the expense of the audience

Facilitator could not balance the group needs with individual needs

Facilitator did not place the method within the larger training context

For Example...

An illustration comes from the author's experience as codirector of a seminar about doing business with Japanese. Attendees at the weekend residential seminar were non-Japanese presidents of Fortune 500 multinational corporations with offices in Tokyo. Both codirectors were on the faculty of an international university in Tokyo. They were being assisted by several Japanese who worked in the corporate context and who were also familiar with intercultural communication. An extensive assessment had been conducted; hundreds of hours of face-to-face interviews had provided the two directors with enough real-time data about the issues and problems faced so that they had created culture assimilators, case studies, and role plays that were direct reflections of the daily realities faced by the participants. The environment was perfect: views of Mt. Fuji and the Pacific Ocean, just the right combination of Japanese food, tatami-mat rooms, and Japanese roommates who also served as the cultural resources for the seminar. All factors were combined so that learning about Japan could occur away from the office but fully within the Japanese context.

After the first evening, participants were asking: "Why are we here?" Obviously, *something* was out of alignment! The seminar began with an explanation of the objectives and history of the project. Wishing to set a frame which emphasized interpersonal communication, the Japanese and non-Japanese introduced themselves to each other in pairs and then were asked to introduce their partner to the entire group. The leaders next held a discussion about different approaches to introductions and the various subjects that are appropriate to reveal and discuss upon meeting a stranger. This was an exercise that both leaders had used repeatedly and successfully with university students. After the discussion, a lavish Japanese dinner was served and participants were free to enjoy more sake, the baths, and a free evening. During dinner, comments from the non-Japanese took the nature of "When is the seminar going to start?" or "I thought this was about business," "I came here to learn about Japanese, not about myself," and "I came here to learn from the experts, not from another person who is as confused as I am."

In the original plan, the following morning was to have begun with a general lecture on intercultural communication, moving into exercises built around culture assimilators and case studies, followed by an evening of films. Role plays were to follow on the third day, building on the assumption that role plays, being potentially more challenging on a personal level, are most effective when participants are more comfortable with the leaders and each other. This plan was completely abandoned. With the help of the Japanese resource persons, the directors, from 10:00 P.M. until 3:00 A.M., received a kind and yet very firm and direct education about "the culture of business." Being the desperate if not quick studies that they were, the directors redesigned the entire seminar so that the next morning the participants were greeted, after morning exercises, with a very different agenda.

The day began with several lectures and films on the history of Japan and the functioning of the political, educational, and social systems as they affect doing business with Japanese. Also included were discussions of factors contributing to the success of multinational corporations in Japan. Following this, intercultural concepts were introduced through case studies and culture assimilators. Role plays began in the evening of the second day and were carried out with volunteers and in private sessions with only the Japanese resource persons and the leaders in attendance.

The participants appreciated the "real" information that was conveyed by "experts." After their expectations about how to learn were met and they became satisfied that their time was going to be used efficiently, they relaxed and enjoyed the real-time nature of the cases and assimilators. These experiences were facilitated so as to create opportunities to discuss concerns and ideas with colleagues and the Japanese resources. As anxieties about "learning anything" were put to rest, they could listen to, and even give legitimacy to, the role of values and perceptions in creating effective interactions. Some even came to appreciate the personal application of the "real information" that could arise during role playing when they realized that they were not being required to perform in front of their colleagues.

Messages

What had been learned? We started out putting our faith in realistic and relevant methodologies and were basing the design on time-tested assumptions relevant to university students about how people can best be drawn in to a learning process. We were as blind as our clients in our out-of-awareness assumptions about how learning should occur and how to create interest and establish rapport. We believed that one must learn first about self in order to be effective in another culture and that an interpersonal focus is the foundation for any effective interaction. All this was carried over from the academic experience and placed directly into a context which did not operate from these assumptions.

There were also important messages heard in the process of redesigning the seminar. While some new content was added, much of the redesign focused on a resequencing of the methods included in the original plan. With acknowledgment of the participants' "business culture," the leaders' styles of delivering material and leading discussion were modified. All of these changes represented a shift in the overall purpose. The leaders were very familiar with the university context in which knowledge and experiences are designed to contribute to the students' process of continual learning. This was neither the context of nor the appropriate process for a business seminar. It was more appropriate to design and deliver knowledge and experiences in a way that contributed to the maximum implementation of the learnings in real business situations. This shift, coupled with the acknowledgment of the different expectation about learning, allowed the redesign to be a relatively easy, though tiring, process.

This seminar occurred in 1978.[14] Today, clients understand more about what can be expected from such experiences and how to evaluate the expertise of professionals in the intercultural field. Intercultural professionals are much more sophisticated about how to design and conduct intercultural learning experiences, the content to be included, and the methodologies through which such content can be conveyed. When taken together, the learning from the above example and the signposts point to similar messages.

Methodologies are highly leader-dependent. Effective leaders use particular methodologies rather than being used by them; effectiveness lies not solely in choosing the "right" case study, role play, or simulation but in the preparation and the attitudes and capabilities of the person guiding the process. Secondly, any method must be context-appropriate. That is, it must be appropriate to the client's requests and to the organization's general situation as well as to the personalities, learning styles, expectations, and experiences of the specific audience. How is such a match achieved? It is necessary to develop purpose and objectives which grow from a thorough understanding of this context. Such an understanding comes from information collected in an assessment of the client's particular situation. From this assessment, content is chosen and methodologies are created.

Needs Assessment

Choices of methodologies are related to information and impressions received through data obtained from a needs assessment. Information is collected about the current reality and about what the client or audience would like their reality to look like. The gap or distance between these views of reality is identified and a learning experience and/or consultation session is designed to facilitate movement in the desired direction. Certainly, identification of the distance or "needs" comes from the client, but it is also very important that we as professionals offer opinions, for, along with increased sophistication and expertise, comes responsibility to more fully educate and more carefully guide those who seek assistance.

An assessment, then, is critical. It is upon the basis of specific data that objectives are set, content and methodologies chosen, the entire experience designed, and evaluations and follow-up carried out. In addition, the process of doing an assessment itself sets expectations and thus can support learning. When the assessment information is shared with participants, they can easily see that their particular situation is not necessarily unique. They can come to understand, as a group, the reality which has given rise to the experience in which they are about to participate.

There are several time-tested techniques for collecting information. Written instruments and interviews are commonly used. Direct observation of meetings, social encounters, and interactions on the manufacturing line or in classrooms are all important in developing an in-depth understanding of what is going on "in reality."

---

[14] John C. Condon and Sheila Ramsey, codirectors; "Pegasus Intercultural Communication Seminar for Non-Japanese Businessmen" sponsored by the International House of Japan and the American Chamber of Commerce in Tokyo; Tokyo, Japan; 1978-1981.

A review of reports, records, and any information that clients publish about themselves is useful to identify their values and norms, i.e., their culture. A quick assessment of participants' expectations and backgrounds at the beginning of a seminar is also important to align what has been learned about a general situation with the specific experiences of the people with whom one will be working. This can also function as a process of setting expectations for the work about to begin. When conducted during a workshop or consultation, such an assessment can provide evaluative feedback vital to assessing how the learning goals are being met.

Most important in relationship to decisions about methods, information collected during an assessment is the basis for creating client-tailored methodologies. With this intent, gathering information about specific situations, problems and confusions, and successes and skills is a necessity. Such information is then used to design free-form exercises, simulations, case studies, or role plays with special attention paid to what degree the scenarios can represent the client's everyday reality. For example, interviews and direct observations of classroom interactions are carried out prior to designing a workshop for teachers entering into a culturally diverse school district. Important issues are identified:

- Students who lack proficiency in English are classified as slow learners.
- Teachers do not understand some students' use of silence.
- Students often don't know what credit and units are needed and don't understand the process for obtaining them.
- Teachers don't understand why some parents of non-U.S.-born students won't come to school; are they afraid of the teacher?
- At recess, students gather with members of their own cultural group; teachers and other students see this in a negative light.[15]

All of this information can find its way into a workshop for new teachers and can be the basis of a range of exercises designed to encourage more and more participant involvement and risk. For example, learning about parents' perceptions of teachers can be first approached through a culture assimilator with given multiple-choice answers. This can be followed with an open-ended case study encouraging more independent in-depth analysis and, finally, can be explored through individual or group role plays in which new teachers are asked to interact with "actors" embodying the parents' and other relatives' values and behaviors.

Clients and audiences today are interested in learning about the difficulties and possibilities of intercultural work through methods which directly address their specific situation rather than relying more heavily on culture-general work. For example, the sales department of an electronics firm prefers case studies or critical incidents to be written about a sales negotiation involving its type of product and client. A firm beginning business in a new culture wants to explore the unfamiliar distribution system; it will actively engage in a role play focusing on the nuances of interactions with a distributor.

---

[15] Example based on the work of Patricia Furey, "A Model for Cross-Cultural Analysis of Teaching Methods." Presentation given at the 14th Annual TESOL Convention, San Francisco, March 1980.

As we set the very important culture-general awareness of value-orientations perception and communication style within such detail and context specificity, we are reminded that our work is a creative process to which we impart a sense of freshness and relevance.

Objectives and Purposes

One of the more difficult experiences for an intercultural trainer or consultant, after having brought a group to the conclusion of a learning experience, is to hear "Excuse me, but I don't understand what just happened; why did we do that?" A first defensive reaction may be one of exasperation with the person who ventured to speak such truth. However, with reflection comes a realization about how the experience was framed. More specifically, one may see that

- o the objectives of the experience were not clear in the mind of the leader,
- o the objectives of the experience were not communicated in ways that could be understood by all,
- o the experience itself was not clearly connected to a bigger picture, i.e., to the client's situation and the larger purpose supporting the need for intercultural work.

As professionals we know the importance of setting objectives. How, then, could this happen? It is important to remember that any well-used or favorite method must be redefined each time it is used. *BaFá BaFá* is one of the most well-known intercultural simulations; it follows a rather set procedure and is accompanied by an instructor's manual outlining the objectives of the simulation. It is easy and tempting to forget that no two simulation experiences are alike. Forgetting this does a disservice to the intricacies of the simulation and the uniqueness of the participants. It becomes important to pay renewed attention to how the objectives can be aligned with the needs and experiences of each audience and how the delivery can be modified.

Even when the objectives are clear in the mind of the consultant or leader, participants listen selectively. The most difficult filters to communicate through are those arising from assumptions about learning. What kind of information is deemed important, new, or useful? In what form does information need to arrive, to be seen as learning? The objectives of an activity or exercise may be stated or shown clearly in the perception of the leader and not be recognized as such or understood by participants. This is more likely to occur if objectives are communicated in only one style or through only one medium.

What of connection to a larger purpose? One may become quite skilled at rapidly turning out objectives for an activity or a program and neglect to position the entire event or session within the larger whole as expressed by, say, a corporate vision statement or the mission of a school district. In other words, is it enough that a simulation results in a variety of "ah ha!" insights and that a two-day workshop received an "outstanding" rating from 95 percent of the participants? If this is the range of our concern, then such feedback is sufficient. However, it is also our responsibility to step outside this narrow focus and ask, "So what?" and "For what?" When managers, doctors, or teachers working as a multicultural team learn skills that can help them communicate more effectively, we must also inquire about and help them to articulate how their new abilities can now support them in serving the greater purposes which have brought them together. Examples of such purpose might include: "creating products that exceed customer expectations while valuing the unique talents of all employees," "educating patients in ways to maintain the highest level of health," or "valuing the diversity of all people in the creation of intercultural partnerships."

As leaders, we must be able to identify, articulate, and hold the objectives of a specific methodology within the objectives of the entire program. All this is then held in alignment with the answers to "So what?" As participants become consciously involved in the creation of this thread of connection, the learning experience has relevance, it makes sense, and, more important, becomes motivating and inspiring.

Content

Earlier in this discussion, it was suggested that intercultural work recycles and re-works a small number of basic themes. These include finding effective ways of living and working with difference, ambiguity, and change as well as accessing creativity and managing one's state of being. Accepting these, an important question arises. When clients and audiences are requesting that intercultural work address very specific situational and culturally specific concerns, how do we incorporate these more general and vitally important themes? This is not a new question, for it is at the heart of the well-known dichotomy between the culture-general and culture-specific approaches to training. What we understand now is that the dichotomy is an illusion. These basic themes are present in all intercultural work, since the work is marked by its concern with diversity. The degree to which such themes are given direct attention is only a function of the intention and skill of the leader. Some methodologies are created to call attention to these themes. The simulation *BaFá BaFá*, for example, calls upon participants to examine their observation skills, how they respond in ambiguous situations and how they learn about others who are quite different from themselves. The multicultural problem-solving simulation *Ecotonos* gives participants the opportunity to explore their creative abilities while working under the constraints of unfamiliar behavioral rules.[16] In other cases, such as a simulation written expressly to teach about decision-making or negotiation styles of Germans or Koreans, these themes are woven into the discussion sessions. In the creation of new methods, it is important to make conscious decisions about how directly these themes will be addressed. Excellent training programs and consultation sessions assist participants in accepting the validity of these themes and in developing related competencies in addition to satisfying participants' needs to understand new culture- and situation-specific ways of living and working.

We know that intercultural competence is a "whole person" experience. It follows that no matter how strong the culture-specific focus of our work, we can only be effective to the degree that we engage the mind, heart, and spirit of those with

---

[16] *Ecotonos: A Multicultural Problem-Solving Simulation,* created by Nipporica Associates (Yarmouth, ME: Intercultural Press, 1992).

whom we work. It is often in relationship to these basic themes that the opportunity for such engagement is present.

Our Role as Professionals

Intercultural work engages all of us, leaders and clients alike, in a journey. Anne Janeway identifies a question that guides us: "…what leads human beings from a state of fear, ignorance, and distrust (if not hatred) of those who are culturally different to a state in which they want to understand, communicate and connect? And once this desire of heart and mind is present, what converts it to action?"[17]

We give shape to this journey not only with the methodologies we choose and create but also with our presence. Should we care to acknowledge and receive it, we are engaged in a service that gives us a gift, that is, the opportunity to align our own abilities and capacities with the work that we choose to do in the world. We have learned to design programs which present culture-specific information. We have become facile in speaking about the importance of self-reflection, about becoming comfortable with ambiguity, about the importance of flexibility, or adapting communication styles. However, these capacities can easily remain conceptual or relegated to a "nice to know and soon forgotten" to-do list unless connected with heart and spirit. In working to bring this connection to life in our counseling sessions or training programs, we are continually called on to manage *our own* state of being, to work with *our own* responses to difference and change, and to access the heights of *our own* creative abilities. Our work is grounded in the very essence of what we are trying to help others bring forth.

Fritjof Capra's film *Mindwalk* addresses the necessity of a new paradigm for survival in today's world. One character declares: "Healing the universe is an inside job."[18] Effective facilitation of intercultural learning experiences is also "an inside job" in that much of the work happens inside of ourselves. As this is so, it becomes our responsibility to continually develop our capacities. A most appropriate brand of in-service education may be to regularly find ways to place ourselves in unknown situations, where differences abound, in which we can not only learn about people of a different culture, but also learn again and again about our own learning style and observation skills and renew our talent for laughing at ourselves. We bring all that we learn in this process of self-renewal to assessing a client's situation, to developing objectives, to choosing content, to creating and using methodologies, and to aligning the entire learning experience with a larger purpose.

---

[17] Anne Janeway, "Beyond Experience: The Experiential Approach to Cross-Cultural Education," in *Beyond Experience*, rev. ed. Edited by Theodore Gochenour (Yarmouth, ME: Intercultural Press, 1993), xvi.

[18] Fritjof Capra, *Mindwalk*, shown during a presentation entitled "The Challenges of the Nineties," Fort Mason Conference Center, San Francisco, August 1992.

Given the status and importance with which intercultural matters are regarded today, it is important for those intimately involved to ask an age-old and ever new set of questions. What are the overall purposes of work undertaken in the name of intercultural communication? How are such purposes in alignment with the global perspectives woven through our local realities? Our personal answers to these questions, consciously pursued, can guide our work and support our commitment to a deeper sense about the role of intercultural communication in the larger perspective.

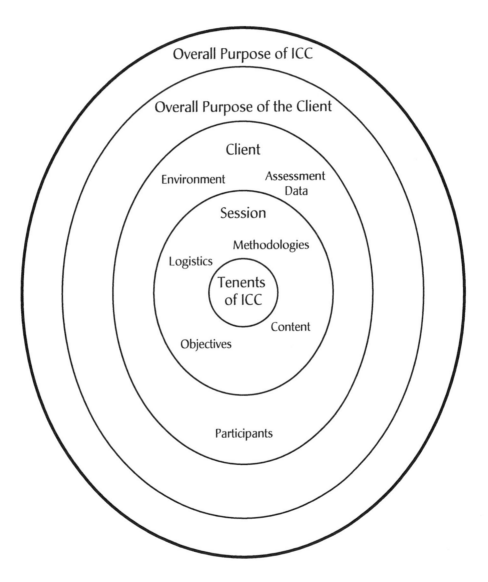

Overall Purpose of ICC

Overall Purpose of the Client

Client

Environment

Assessment Data

Session

Methodologies

Logistics

Tenents of ICC

Content

Objectives

Participants

So What?

Our decisions about the methodologies we create and use are framed within the shape of our world—the basic tenets of the intercultural field—and are given character by such building blocks as the process of assessment and the careful attention we must pay to objectives and content. Our relationship to methodologies is highly personal and dynamic and, therefore, creative. The beliefs we hold about the purposes of our work and the role intercultural education has to play in today's world are evident in our creations.

In psychology and communication, a basic definition of dysfunction is related to interpreting events using a narrow frame of reference. From studies in ecology and genetics, we learn that having limited ways to respond to crises is life-threatening. Intercultural education reminds us that not honoring diversity is a decision we make at our own risk. As we continue to learn about working and living well within a human ecology of diversity which is our source of hope and creativity, we are continually challenged to accept our role as creators of our global experience.

Section I: Getting into Focus (activities 1-4)

Introduction

How would you explain to a fish who has never been outside of water what water is? Since it knows nothing else, it cannot in any objective sense know even the one thing it thinks it knows—water. Maybe the fish doesn't even think about water until out of it. Only when the fish feels what it is like to move in air's less viscous environment, breathing in oxygen from a nonliquid source, does the fish realize the properties of water that it has taken for granted all its life.

Likewise, people who have not experienced what it is like to live in a culture with different ground rules governing thought and behavior need to get a sense of the properties of the cultural air in which they are immersed. Air, like water to fish, is invisible; what is detectable is its effect on things, such as when it moves clouds or bends trees. How do we give culturally naive individuals a sense of culture's consequence?

We could, of course, explain it to them. But, as Confucius has observed, one picture is worth a whole lot of words. The first three activities in this section follow the advice of Confucius. They provide one with visual images that allow our companions in learning (i.e., our students or trainees) to see the effects of conditioning on our perception. In the first activity by Gary R. Smith and George G. Otero, "Behind Our Eyes," it is the internal neurological structures of our bodies that lead us to deny reality. In Ann Hubbard's clever activity "The Zebra's Stripes," it is prior context that determines how outside reality is perceived. Prior context becomes, conveniently, the analogue of one's native culture. Thomas Baglan presents us with another visual image in "A Cube Is a Cube…." Here, Baglan takes a Euclidian image that is relatively devoid of cultural "loadings," unlike other geometric images such as a star or a cross that often evoke rich cultural associations, and invites the student to see it from various perspectives. The analogy is that each view of the cube represents a different worldview.

The final activity of this section was selected because it innovatively departs from the teacher-as-facilitator paradigm. Jane Stewart Heckman, Mary J. H. Beech, and Louise Munns Kuzmarskis provide a technique that culturally naive people can adopt to teach themselves about cross-cultural topics. The particular examples that the authors present involve how to go about organizing study groups on women's global issues. Women's issues are certainly relevant to the field of intercultural communication. As the editor of the book in which an earlier draft of this exercise appears puts it: "For thinking to be truly global, it must take into account the thoughts and experiences of women." The format these authors outline can easily be adapted to virtually any topic.

1

Behind Our Eyes
Gary R. Smith and George G. Otero

There is a Chinese proverb that says, "We see what is behind our eyes." This activity introduces the concept of perception with a set of drawings. The idea it presents is that how our brains process the information causes us to perceive objects the way we do.

Objectives

1. From a variety of visual displays, describe how context and background affect the way figures are perceived.
2. Without references, generate at least one hypothesis concerning the implication of misperceiving other people.
3. From one's context, generate at least two examples of perception and misperception not previously discussed.

Grade Level

2–12. (For children in grade school, the questions suggested under Procedure, below, would have to be simplified.)

Time

25–30 minutes.

Materials

Handout: Ten Figures, chalkboard, and chalk.

Procedure

Step 1. Write the proverb on the chalkboard, "We see what is behind our eyes."

Step 2. Ask students to explain what they think the proverb means. Don't spend too much time on this. There will be opportunity in the next step for further discussion. Distribute the handout to students.

Step 3. Explain that Figures 1 through 10 on the handout illustrate one interpretation of the proverb. Here is a guide for taking participants through the drawings on the handout:

Fig. 1: Which one of the two horizontal lines is longer?

Answer: Both lines are the same length. What causes us to be misled is not clearly understood. Psychologists tell us that we are influenced by the other lines in the drawing (context) which lead us to make wrong guesses about what we perceive. Even though we know the answer, our eyes tell us differently.

Fig. 2: Are the horizontal lines straight?

Answer: Yes, even though they appear to be bent. The illusion is caused, in part, by our interpretation of the lines in context with the other lines.

Fig. 3: Are the horizontal lines straight?

Answer: Yes. (Same reason as given for Figure 2.)

Fig. 4: Does the square have straight sides or are they bowed inward?

Answer: The square has straight sides, even though we perceive them as being bowed.

Fig. 5: Is the cube facing left or right?

Answer: Either way. Our perceptions keep changing!

Fig. 6: Which way through the coils—left or right?

Answer: Either way. Our perceptions keep changing.

Fig. 7: Do you see a flight of stairs or a decorative overhang?

Answer: Either.

Fig. 8: Do you perceive movement in this drawing?

Answer: Most people do because of the involuntary movement of the eye.

Fig. 9: Is this a "possible" figure or an "impossible" one? Follow the stairs around and try to determine whether they're going up or down.

Fig. 10: Is this a possible figure or an impossible one? Try to imagine what the triangle would look like in a three-dimensional plane.

Follow-up

1. Pick out a few of the drawings and see if you can deduce a central theme about them. (Perhaps "Seeing is not believing.")

2. How do you explain why you might be fooled by some of the figures, if you have not seen them before or "gotten the point" of the activity?

3. Can you suggest what the Chinese proverb means after having looked at the drawings? (One possible interpretation is that the source of illusions and mis-perceptions must be sought in the brain, not in the senses.)

4. Explain the statement, "Context or background affects the way we perceive things."

5. Suggest some problems that might arise when you misperceive other people.

6. Ask participants to create hypotheses about how visual perception might affect cultural understanding. List these hypotheses on the chalkboard or butcher paper. Some hypotheses which might be generated are:

   o what we perceive can be misleading

   o perceptions depend on context, particularly cultural context

   o different people have different perceptions of the same stimulus, and all perceptions may be equally valid

7. Ask participants to brainstorm other instances in which perception plays an important part. List these on the board or paper.

Further Reading

Escher, M. C., and J. L. Locher. *The World of M. C. Escher*. New York: Harry N. Abrams, 1971.

Hall, Edward T. "Context and Meaning." In *Beyond Culture*, Chapter 6. New York: Doubleday, 1976.

Morris, Charles G. "Perception." In *Psychology: An Introduction*, 7th ed., Chapter 9. Englewood Cliffs, NJ: Prentice-Hall, 1990.

This activity is taken from Gary R. Smith and George G. Otero, *Teaching about Cultural Awareness*. Denver, CO: Center for Teaching International Relations, University of Denver, 1977.

Handout: Ten Figures

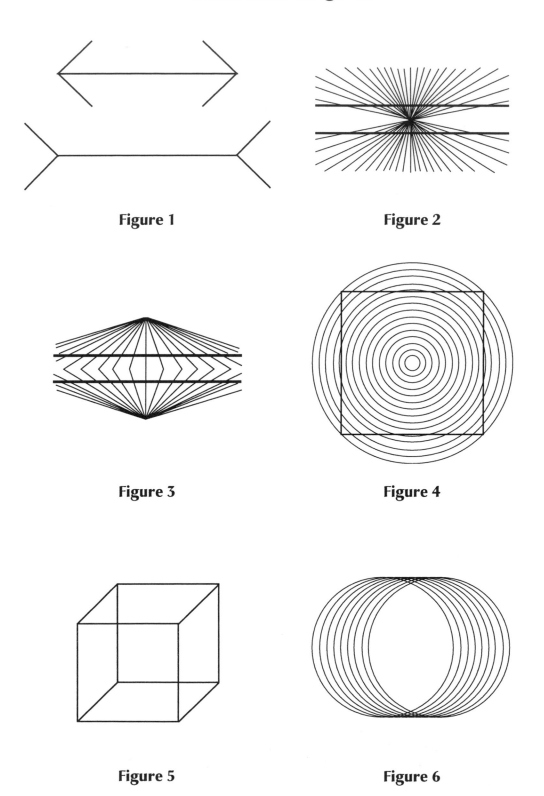

Figure 1

Figure 2

Figure 3

Figure 4

Figure 5

Figure 6

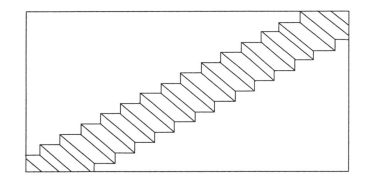

Figure 7

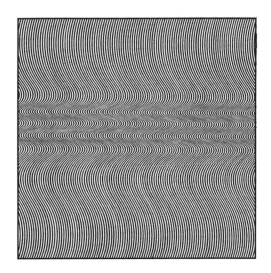

Figure 8

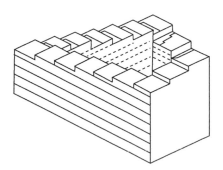

Figure 9

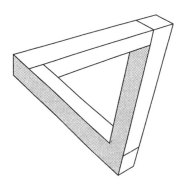

Figure 10

The Zebra's Stripes
Ann Hubbard

Objectives
To illustrate how context is one of the determinants of selective perception; to demonstrate how culturally programmed orientations lead to differing points of view.

Materials
Student Handout: The Zebra's Stripes (or transparencies of each handout page for the overhead projector).

Procedure
1. Have half the students step outside the room.
2. Show image #1 of the zebra to the students remaining in the classroom. Allow them to look at the picture for no more than 10 seconds. Ask them: "What color are the zebra's stripes?"
3. Have the two groups of students switch places.
4. Show image #2 of the zebra to the group of students now in the classroom. Ask them to look at the picture for no more than 10 seconds. Ask them: "What color are the zebra's stripes?"
5. Have both groups of students come together. Show image #3 of the zebra. Ask the students what color the zebra's stripes are. Those who saw image #1 probably will answer "black." Those who saw image #2 probably will answer "white."

It is claimed that while people in the United States generally consider the zebra to be a white animal with black stripes, most Africans consider it to be a black animal with white stripes (Berlitz, C., *Native Tongues*. New York: Putnam, 1982).

Discussion Questions
○ If members of each group respond differently about the color of the zebra's stripes, discuss how and why this happened. Show students the difference in the three zebras.

o If the second group saw that the zebra had black stripes, why did this happen? Could they be culturally conditioned to believe that the zebra's stripes are black?

o How can people of one culture claim that the zebra's stripes are black, while people in another culture claim they are white?

o What is perception? How does our visual perception affect the way we process information about the world around us and the way we form attitudes, etc.?

Discussion

The concept of perception is one with which intercultural trainers often begin in order to show the different ways in which people process information and images. This example is intended to show a parallel to how we process information about other groups of people and form stereotypes. Not only do we carefully select what we see or think, but we often have trouble shifting to a different view.

There are many reasons why we don't all perceive things in the same way—from physical differences when perceiving visual images to past experiences and culturally conditioned attitudes. This simple exercise may be accompanied by others on perception (see resources below), or used as a lead-in to exercises in other training areas (defining culture, values, etc.)

Tips

Trainers should not ignore the fact that some people can become very frustrated by simple exercises such as these (e.g., by being unable to see in an image what everyone else in the group *can* see). Care should be taken not to make anyone feel stupid in these situations. Even with such a seemingly nonthreatening example as the color of a zebra's stripes, people can become significantly disturbed when confronted with a different viewpoint. They may also simply not get it. Following the debriefing of this exercise one day, a U.S. college student raised her hand and asked, "But the zebra's stripes really *are* black, aren't they?"

Further Reading

Pusch, M., ed. *Multicultural Education: A Cross-Cultural Training Approach*. Yarmouth, ME: Intercultural Press, 1979.

Smith, G., and G. Otero. *Teaching about Cultural Awareness*. Denver, CO: Center for Teaching International Relations, University of Denver, 1986.

Handout: The Zebra's Stripes

Illustration by Charles Hubbard.

Illustration by Charles Hubbard.

Illustration by Charles Hubbard.

A Cube Is a Cube...

Thomas Baglan

Objective

To allow participants to experience the effects of viewing the world in one way and then attempting to change that view.

Participants

Any number.

Materials

A place for the facilitator to draw a large cube, or a poster with a cube drawn on it.

Setting

No special requirements.

Time

20–40 minutes.

Procedure

1. Begin by drawing a cube on the blackboard, similar to the one below:

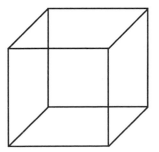

2. Inform students that there are two ways to view the cube: (a) the cube can be viewed as if it were facing downward, i.e., the front face of the cube appears to be downward and to the left, as if the cube were being viewed from above; (b) the cube can be viewed as if it were facing upward, i.e., the front face of the cube appears to be upward and to the right, as if the cube were being viewed from below.

3. Allow the students a minute or two to try to visualize the cube from each of these perspectives. Inform them that both perspectives are legitimate ways of seeing the cube.

4. Have the students imagine that they live in a culture where everyone sees upward-facing cubes. Instruct them to visualize the cube in that way. While they are doing that, say something like the following:

> Imagine that you live in a culture in which everyone sees the cube in only one way, i.e., as if it is facing upward. In this culture, cubes have achieved great symbolic significance, similar to symbols in our own culture, like the cross or the flag. The symbol of the cube is depicted in many areas, such as advertising or television, as are symbols in our culture. Indeed, great works of art depict upward-facing cubes, and the properties and significance of upward-facing cubes are discussed by scholars in many disciplines. The cubes have achieved a prominent status to the extent that they are objects of research, objects of philosophical discussion, works of art, etc.

> Someone growing up in such a culture would have difficulty seeing the cube in any other way. If an outsider suggested that the cube could be viewed differently, that suggestion would be heard with disbelief. After viewing the cube in this way for a couple of minutes, it is indeed difficult to change one's perceptions.

5. Have the students imagine that they now live in a culture where everyone sees downward-facing cubes. Instruct them to now view the cube in this manner. It may take a minute to change their perceptions of the cube. Again, while they are viewing the cube in this way, describe a culture in which the downward-facing cube has achieved great significance and is studied and written about by the greatest minds of the culture. After viewing the cube in this way for a couple of minutes, it is difficult to view it in any other way.

6. Imagine an encounter between two individuals, one who had grown up in the first hypothetical culture and one who had grown up in the second. The views of each would seem wrong to the other. Perhaps one or both would be accused of heresy. Perhaps, if the feelings were strong enough, a heated argument or even a fight would ensue.

7. Present an analogy between views of the cube and worldviews of different cultures. A worldview seems correct to the members of a culture who hold that view. Since the worldview of a culture is held unconsciously and accepted without question by large numbers of people, alternate views may seem wrong.

8. Now inform the students that there really is no cube on the board at all since cubes are three-dimensional and the blackboard is two-dimensional. Instruct them to try to visualize the drawing as an abstract pattern of lines in two-dimensional space. They may have difficulty seeing this, but will be able to understand intellectually that what is on the board is not really a cube since cubes are three-dimensional. Inform them that both ways of previously viewing the cube, i.e., as upward-facing or downward-facing, were in a sense both legitimate yet neither was more true than the other. In another sense, both were incomplete views since in fact no cube existed.

Another analogy can be made with regard to worldviews. Each worldview is a legitimate yet incomplete way of perceiving things. The view of the cube facing upward and the view of the cube facing downward are not contradictory views; they are complementary. Each provides an aspect that the other lacks. The same is true of worldviews. Each provides a way of seeing that is not present in another. Each is partially accurate, yet none is completely true.

Discussion

Such descriptions of hypothetical cultures may sound farfetched, but in our own culture we have symbols which have achieved such prominence, e.g., the cross, the flag, corporate logos, etc.

Since the student's visual attention is focused on the cubes during the description of the hypothetical cultures, the desired effect of viewing something in one way and then finding it difficult to change that view is produced.

The advantage of using a cube is that there are generally no existing connotations associated with cubes as there would be with other more familiar symbols. This seems to help in stimulating students' imagination during the exercise.

Theoretical Framework/Rationale

The worldview of a culture is generally not explicitly taught, but rather learned implicitly through the process of socialization. It is generally accepted without question. The manner in which it is taught and the absence of critical questioning leads to a situation in which the members of a culture usually cannot articulate their own worldview. Therefore, to discuss one's own worldview or that of another culture is generally a difficult matter. The worldview is usually held unconsciously yet influences the attitudes, perceptions, values, and behaviors of the members of a culture.

This exercise helps students to understand some important facts about the worldview: (1) even though our worldview may be held unconsciously, it affects our values and perceptions; (2) each worldview is a legitimate way of perceiving the world even though it is only partially accurate; and (3) different worldviews are not contradictory but complementary.

Trainer Tips

It helps if the concept of worldview and the purposes which a worldview serves in a culture are presented prior to doing the exercise. I also ask students if they can articulate their worldview—most cannot and indeed have never even thought about doing so. Yet the worldview which they hold influences their attitudes, values, behaviors, perceptions, etc.

I am always struck by the inability of many students to view the cube in one way after looking at it in the other way for only a couple of minutes. This makes it very easy for them to understand how difficult it can be to "see" another's worldview. After growing up in one culture under the influence of a particular worldview, it is very easy to label a different one as wrong. Discussion of this exercise seems to center around these issues.

Further Reading

I like the discussion of worldviews in W. B. Gudykunst and Y. Y. Kim, *Communicating with Strangers: An Approach to Intercultural Communication,* Reading, MA: Addison-Wesley, 1984.

4

Organizing Self-Directed Study Groups on Women's Global Issues

Jane Stewart Heckman, Mary J. H. Beech, and Louise Munns Kuzmarskis

Objective

To present a plan for organizing self-directed study groups on global issues.

Participants

Any number, any ages.

Materials

Books, articles, films, filmstrips, audiotapes or cassette discs, and recipes according to the group members' interests and time.

Setting

No special requirements.

Time

Variable: perhaps 2 hours per meeting.

Background

A seminar, "Global Thinking on Local Issues: Focusing on the Personal, National and International Connections in Women's Lives," was designed by and for a group of women working through the YWCA of Metropolitan Chicago and funded in part by a grant from the Illinois Humanities Council in 1984-1985. Our goals were to expand our awareness of global issues affecting women, to develop a working knowledge of the conditions under which women live, and to network with others on the implications of these global issues for local action. The study series of six sessions provided an opportunity for women to examine these ideas with academic humanists and with women whose international background and life experience provided a personal dimension that encouraged empathy. This article sets out ways to create a study group with or without academic and international resource persons.

Why Study Women's Global Issues?

"While women represent half the global population and one-third of the labor force, they receive only one-tenth of the world income and own less than 1 percent of world property. They are responsible for two-thirds of all working hours." This oft-repeated quote from Kurt Waldheim's "Report to the UN Commission on the Status of Women" (the statistics are from Development Issue, Paper No. 12, UNDP, cited in *Sisterhood Is Global*) points to both the significant contributions of women and their relative lack of power. Few general books on world history, international relations, or economic development provide equitable coverage of women's contributions. Yet there are literally thousands of subject-specific books, journals, articles, films, and videos documenting the importance of women's contributions to the global economy and to the world's art, literature, and music. It's time to apprise ourselves of these offerings.

Procedure

1. Form a group.

   The first step in initiating a self-directed study group is to gather a group of people who share an interest in knowing more about women in international perspective. If the direction of the group is to be shared and "owned" by all participants, it is important to include everyone in the planning phase. Having one or a few interested persons set up a program and assume responsibility will be more efficient in the short run, but is unlikely to result in investment in the program by other participants. Call each person individually to invite her to participate in planning a study group and then follow up with a written reminder of the time and place of the planning meeting. Contact as diverse a group as possible to join the study group in order to elicit life stories and perspectives that cross class, race, religious and national differences. Try to balance participants from different countries, classes, and/or religious, ethnic, or racial groups, so as to avoid making some group members feel they are "tokens."

2. Introduce the basic idea at an organizational meeting.

   For this type of self-directed study group, it is valuable to begin with an organizational meeting to introduce the basic ideas behind establishing the group. Two short videos, "Child of the Universe" (5 min.) and "No More Separate Futures" (9 min.),[1] can be used to focus the group's attention on the relevance of global issues. Small-group discussions, after the videos, enable the participants to begin to think about the ideas stimulated by the presentation. The organizers of this introductory meeting can provide a few questions to initiate consid-

---

[1] Available from Church World Service Film Library, see "Catalogues" under Resources.

eration of what the group wants to find out about women's lives around the world.

3. Divide the group into topic teams.

   The general plan for the study group is presented by the initiator and discussed by the group. We suggest that, at the opening organizing meeting, the group divide itself into five or six teams, one for each major topic of the series. Each member chooses a topic in which she is especially interested (or a second or third choice so that subgroups are about equal in size). Each team then accepts responsibility for planning the presentation and discussion of its chosen topic at one of the subsequent meetings of the total group. The selection of specific topics should be made according to the interests of the group members. Sessions may focus on a nation or region of the world as well as, or alternating with, a women's issue. The topics selected by the YWCA group were:

   Women and the Military-Industrial Complex

   Women, Multinationals, and Economic Development

   Women and Food, Land, and Hunger

   Women and Work

   Women and Violence

4. Each team prepares and presents a topic.

   A self-directed study group divides responsibility for intensive participation among all members of the group. Each person then has a major responsibility with her teammates for one meeting and also participates by doing some background reading for all meetings and for discussion at the sessions. The team responsible for presentation of a topic should read additional references in addition to the basic reading and contribute some of that knowledge to the group. All, however, will read the basic articles so that they can be prepared to participate in the group discussion.

5. Use several media, stimulate several senses.

   The teams may use a variety of methods for presentation of their topics including maps, a video, film or filmstrip, an exercise or simulation, a panel discussion, a role play or brief presentations by international participants or local scholars specializing in the study of women's lives internationally. Fiction, in the form of short stories, novels, or poetry, and memoirs by women writers often promote identification with women living in a specific country or culture in ways that statistics and essays may not. Consider including these as part of the study-group reading or as an alternative focus. Music, art, posters, photographs, and cartoons by and about women as well as snacks from the same region of the world will expand the sensory impact of a group's presentation. The formal program should take no more than one hour and preferably less. Allow several weeks between the organizing session and the first session of the study series for each team to gather materials, prepare its presentation, and provide readings for the rest of the group.

6. Provide time for discussion.

   Don't overprogram the sessions. Remember, some of your great ideas can be used in a second round of reading and self-study sessions. A major portion of each session is needed to provide time for all members of the group to participate in the discussion. Too much presentation puts us back into the passive mode of observers or spectators. Enough time needs to be allotted for basic facts and figures to be presented and understood, lest the discussion reflect no more than preformed attitudes. And enough time needs to be allotted for active discussion of each topic so that everyone has the opportunity to voice her ideas, to be heard and responded to by others in the group.

7. Update what's going on in the community.

   We found it very useful to allow some time at the beginning of each session for announcements of events related to women's issues locally and globally and for information on upcoming legislation. One group found it enjoyable to have a vegetarian potluck supper before the presentation and discussion to allow for fellowship and networking.

8. Speakers enhance study groups.

   Outside speakers can indeed have an audience-drawing appeal and often have considerable knowledge of the topic being discussed. A short series of speakers or an occasional guest speaker can stimulate new types of thinking by group members. Speakers can also add alternative viewpoints to the deliberations of the group. On the other hand, an overreliance on one or a few experts for the interpretation of world events can be a facile shortcut for working through our own analyses of these issues. Reliance on experts can also undermine one's trust in the knowledge and experience of the participants. Thus, even if funding is available or qualified "experts" are willing to donate their time, a lecture is no substitute for systematic study of a subject and becoming informed on something as complex as global interdependence. So if your group does not have access to speakers, study first and seek out the experts later.

9. Encourage and value diverse perspectives.

   We cannot stress too strongly the benefits of including international participants in a seminar where the focus is women's lives around the world. Women who have grown up in other countries bring with them different perspectives on womanhood and on virtually every other aspect of life. Their perspectives, like ours, were formed through childhood experiences in the family, among friends, and within systems of formal education. Unlike many of us, they have had the jolting experience of having many of their cultural assumptions questioned by foreigners such as ourselves who grew up in different environments. Since our goal is to acquire a global perspective, a diversity of national, ethnic, racial, and economic backgrounds among the seminar participants is a logical, but easily overlooked, starting point.

10. Recognize the group's own homogeneity and other limitations.

    If the participants are mainly from one race, speak only one language, are of about the same age, are from the same socioeconomic class, and from similar religious and ethnic backgrounds, there is likely to be a similar perspective which will limit the ability to "see," "hear," and understand other perspectives. It may be possible to recruit a diverse group of women to participate, but if the group is homogeneous, this needs, at least, to be recognized as a limitation.

Whatever the composition of the group, encourage the expression of a diversity of opinions and perspectives. The world is full of fantastic women and there are thousands of great resources available to enable us to know them. Enjoy getting acquainted!

Resources on Women in International Perspective

Study Action Manual

Heckman, Jane Stewart, Mary J. H. Beech, and Louise Munns Kuzmarskis. 1985. *Global Thinking on Local Issues: A Study-Action Manual.* Chicago: YWCA of Metropolitan Chicago. This manual, from which the above has been excerpted (8-10) and revised, includes theoretical perspectives, exercises, and suggestions for resource materials for each of the topics discussed. For availability of this manual contact Mary J. H. Beech, 736 N. Humphrey Ave., Oak Park, IL 60302.

Books: Facts and Analysis

The following books give an overview of women in the world as a whole. There are many additional resources available focusing on women in one world region.

Albrecht, Lisa, and Rose M. Brewer, eds. *Bridges of Power: Women's Multicultural Alliances.* Santa Cruz, CA: New Society Publishers, 1990.

Duley, Margot I., and Mary I. Edwards, eds. *The Cross-Cultural Study of Women.* New York: Feminist Press, 1986.

Enloe, Cynthia. *The Morning After: Sexual Politics at the End of the Cold War.* Berkeley: University of California Press, 1994.

Gallagher, Margaret, and Lilia Quindoza-Santiago. *Women Empowering Communication: A Resource Book on Women and the Globalization of Media.* New York: International Women's Tribune Center, Isis International, and World Association for Christian Communication, 1994.

International Labour Standards and Women Workers: Information Kit. Includes video (18 min.) and six posters as well as brochures and directory. New York: International Labor Office, 1993. Available through Women, Ink, 777 United Nations Plaza, New York, NY 10017.

Mohanty, Chandra Talpade, Ann Russo, and Lourdes Torres, eds. *Third World Women and the Politics of Feminism.* Bloomington, IN: Indiana University Press, 1991.

Morgan, Robin, ed. *Sisterhood Is Global.* Garden City, NY: Doubleday, 1984.

Mosse, Julia Cleves. *Half the World, Half a Chance.* New York: Oxfam Publications, 1993.

Rao, Aruna, ed. *Women's Studies International: Nairobi and Beyond.* New York: Feminist Press, 1991.

Seager, Joni, and Ann Olson. *Women in the World: An International Atlas.* New York: Simon & Schuster Touchstone Books, 1986. This book uses 1980 statistics and is now out of print, but the maps make a trip to your library to find it worthwhile.

Sivard, Ruth Leger. *Women...A World Survey.* Washington, DC: World Priorities, 1985.

Tomasevski, Katarina. *Women and Human Rights.* New York: Zed Books, 1993.

Waring, Marilyn. *If Women Counted: A New Feminist Economics.* San Francisco: Harper and Row, 1988.

The World's Women 1970-1990: Trends and Statistics. New York: UN Publications, 1991.

Young, Gay, Vidyanali Samarasinghe, and Ken Kusterer, eds. *Women at the Center: Development Issues and Practices for the 1990s.* West Hartford, CT: Kumarian Press, 1993.

Fiction

Arkin, Marian, and Barbara Shollar, eds. *Longman Anthology of World Literature by Women 1875-1975.* New York: Longman, 1989. Short stories and excerpts. Regional essays on women's literary traditions are excellent. Indexes by region and writer.

Bankier, Joanna, et al., eds. *The Other Voice: Twentieth-Century Women's Poetry in Translation.* Foreword by Adrienne Rich. New York: W. W. Norton, n.d.

Busby, Margaret, ed. *Daughters of Africa: An International Anthology of Words and Writings by Women of African Descent from the Ancient Egyptian to the Present.* New York: Pantheon, 1992. Stories, poetry, excerpts. Short biographies. Excellent list of sources on authors. Indexes by country, author.

Correas de Zapata, Celia, ed. *Short Stories by Latin American Women: The Magic and the Real.* Houston: Arte Publico Press, 1989.

Cosman, Carol, Joan Keefe, and Kathleen Weaver, eds. *The Penguin Book of Women Poets.* New York: Penguin Books, 1978.

Gilbert, Sandra M., and Susan Gubar, eds. *The Norton Anthology of Literature by Women: The Tradition in English.* New York: W. W. Norton, 1985. Short stories, excerpts, poetry. Excellent introductory essays. Selected bibliographies.

Penelope, Julia, and Sarah Valentine, eds. *International Feminist Fiction.* Freedom, CA: Crossing Press, 1992. Short biographical notes on authors.

Journals

Connexions: An International Women's Quarterly. Available from Peoples Translations Service, Connexions, PO Box 14431, Berkeley, CA 94701; phone: (510) 549-3505. Short selections on a topic, often written in the first person from contributors around the world.

DAWN. Available from Peggy Antrobus, Director of Women and Development, School of Continuing Study, University of the West Indies, St. Michael, Barbados, West Indies. A newsletter on the impact of global economics on all of us.

Ms. Available from Ms, PO Box 57118, Boulder, CO 80321-7118. Each issue includes a section of international news on women.

Women's Studies International Forum. Available from Pergamon Press, 660 White Plains Road, Tarrytown, NY 10591-5153. Internet "ppi@pergamon.com." Academic research on women's issues.

Catalogues

"Books on Women and Development." Books on women and development from the United Nations and many presses. Available free from Women, Ink., International Women's Tribune Centre, 777 United Nations Plaza, New York, NY 10017; phone (212) 687-8633; fax (212) 661-2704.

"Film and Video Catalogue." Films by women film and video makers. Includes major section on "Global Perspectives & Cultural Identity." Updated annually. Often expensive to rent, but titles may be available through local or community college video libraries. Available from Women Make Movies, Inc., Order Department, 462 Broadway, Suite 500, New York, NY 10013; phone (212) 925-0606; fax (212) 925-2052.

"Free Loan Audiovisual Resources." A catalogue of videos, films, and filmstrips on issues of global hunger, economic development, human rights, the environment, war and peacemaking, and women's issues, including many focused on a particular nation. Materials are available for use free, except for the cost of prompt return by UPS. Catalogue available from Church World Service Film Library, PO Box 968, 28606 Phillips Street, Elkhart, IN 46515; phone (219) 264-3102; fax (219) 262-0966.

"Music by Women." Music by women from around the world, including the United States. Updated two to three times per year. Available free from Ladyslipper, PO Box 3124, Durham, NC 27715; phone (800) 634-6044; fax (919) 682-5601.

Section II: Knowing Yourself as a Cultural Person (activities 5–10)

Introduction

Knowing yourself (Socrates' admonition) is never easy. When faced with the option of fathoming the cultural origin of your own cherished values and beliefs or of learning about the quaint worldview of someone from another culture, people interested in cultural dynamics almost invariably choose the latter. It is just too painful to see ourselves to any extent as Pavlovian dogs trained to salivate at culture's call. It is easy to see other people that way, though. We have little inhibition about making cultural generalities that explain the behavior of people from other societies. Walt Kelly's Okeefenoke Swamp cartoon character, Pogo, has it right: "We have met the enemy and he is us."

This section offers six tools to facilitate an understanding that we are all the product of our society's learned conventions.

The first tool (or activity), Ruth Lambach's "What's in a Name?," is an icebreaker where participants talk about their names, adding cultural observations where appropriate. For instance, in some cultures the "last name" appears first (China, Japan), or next to last (Hispanic cultures). In cases where a different alphabet or writing system is used in the participant's home country, the participant's name is written on the board in this transcription too.

The second tool was designed by Indrei Ratiu to help participants see the distinction between people (and cultures) who need to analyze a lot of explicit information before reaching a decision and those who intuit their direction from inexplicit, amorphous data. He bases the activity on Edward T. Hall's descriptions of "low-context" and "high-context" cultures. Methodologically, Ratiu presents the participants with a conceptual frame and they deduce how the high- versus low-context distinction affects everyday behavior.

Donald W. Klopf, in the third tool, provides an "Intercultural Self-Disclosure Scale." The participants are asked how much they disclose themselves to their mother, father, lover, friend, culture acquaintance, and culture stranger across thirty topics (organized under opinions, interests and tastes, work and/or studies, money, personality, and body). The facilitator then leads the participants in a discussion of how they would handle a situation where the other person has a different idea of what should be shared.

A clinical psychologist, Jorge Cherbosque, provides the fourth tool, "The Magic Box." Participants choose one of their multiple identities (race/ethnicity, gender, occupation, physical characteristic, religion), think of a negative stereotype associated with it, then gather in a circle to play a variation of "spin the bottle." When the bottle points at an individual, that person talks about the stereotype he or she has identified. After all the participants have had a chance to talk, the facilitator asks them to get rid of the stereotype by identifying someone they personally know who contradicts the stereotype.

The tool for gaining insight into how cultural traditions shape values is proverbs—everyperson's bite-sized bits of culturally transmitted wisdom. Sandra Tjitendero presents five interesting proverbs and asks the participants to think of parallel proverbs in their own culture, and then to try to guess the culture of origin of the five original proverbs. L. Robert Kohls adds a variation on this exercise by inviting participants to list cultural proverbs and then to discuss which of them may no longer apply to mainstream society and why.

5

What's in a Name?

Ruth Lambach

Objective

Break the ice, establish rapport, and engage people with each other easily by focusing on their names. This exercise is designed to create a sense of community in the classroom or among any varied group of people gathered for a common purpose.

Participants

From 3 to 30 people, ideally around 20.

Materials

Blackboard and chalk or large sheets of paper and magic markers.

Time

Depending on the number of people involved, this can take 10-90 minutes.

Procedure

1. The facilitator goes to the board and demonstrates first. (The climate established in this demonstration is the key to the exercise.) Those who follow will take their cue from the self-revelations of the facilitator. I go to the board and write out my name, Ruth Baer Lambach. I usually begin by saying: "When I was about four years old I wanted to change my name because the other children could not pronounce it well. "Ruth" came out sounding like "Fuss" which in German means "foot." One morning while my mother was braiding my hair I told her I wanted to change my name. She told me that would be expensive. I asked "How much?" She told me $500. I knew there wasn't that much in my piggy bank so I was stuck with my name…. I continue telling stories about my maiden name Baer and how it was that none of my thirteen siblings nor I had a middle name…. Sometimes I repeat other short Biblical names and sometimes I don't. My story varies depending on the length of time, number of people, time of day, and how expansive I feel.

2. My name is left on the board and I give the chalk to an alert-looking student or ask for a volunteer who then goes up and does the same.

3. No names are erased. Each person gets to be identified on the board. This exercise never fails to work. People find it easy to talk about a topic about which they are the expert. This gives them confidence. The speaker, by focusing on the name which is written on the board, is relieved of a certain self-conscious anxiety. Sometimes there are questions from the audience to the person at the board. This leads to interesting exchanges and little-known facts about other cultures and their naming practices.

Discussion

This exercise can go on for an hour without signs of boredom.

In the process, the facilitator develops a better grasp of the nature of his or her audience and by offering responses and encouraging interactions can establish an atmosphere of spontaneity within a structured class setting.

Participants, no matter how different their backgrounds, all share in having a family which named them. This common feature helps to establish a sense of community.

At a recent presentation with a group of high school teachers, one of them, as soon as I sat down, commented: "You want us to follow that act?" Later, after everyone had identified themselves, I confronted her in front of the whole group about why she thought it was a contest. We were able to discuss this question with a greater degree of honesty than we would have otherwise had we not spent 45 minutes sharing something quite personal with each other. It is at once personal and public, since everyone has a personal name one uses to present oneself in public.

This exercise can be even more interesting if some of your participants come from countries with different orthographic systems such as Arabic, Russian, Greek, Chinese, Japanese, or Korean. Sometimes shy by cultural inclination or because of what they believe to be inadequate English, they can be drawn naturally in to the group process by giving them the chance to amaze their fellow participants with their mastery of an "arcane" writing system.

The exercise can be varied to accommodate the audience. I have used it with beginning language learners and with a group of managers at one of Chicago's largest corporations. In language classes, simply getting students up to the board and speaking up clearly enough for others to hear them is an accomplishment. With adults or in the corporate setting it is an invariably effective icebreaker. Whenever and wherever I use it, I am struck by how the dynamics in the room change once each of the participants has been identified in this way. While the amount of self-exposure is small, there is a risk when they go to the board. This combination seems to help people move beyond being strangers and quickly open productive channels of communication.

If you are adept at memorization, facing the group after everyone's name is on the board and rapidly rattling off their names brings the exercise to an enjoyable conclusion. Often a participant is willing and able to do this.

Optional Ending

One way to extend the exercise is to help participants pair up with a person with whom they think they have the least in common, the most in common, someone they would like to know better, or someone from a different country or culture.

6

"Facts" or "Feel"?

Indrei Ratiu

Objective

To understand that some people—and some cultures—require a great deal more information than others to make a decision. That is, some people and cultures are "low-context" while others are "high-context."

Participants

Any number of adults (to make appropriate for younger people, change the wording, especially of the items in Handout 3).

Materials

Pencils. Three handouts.

Time

1-2 hours, depending on group size.

Procedures

1. Pass out Handout 1. Ask readers to note the main characteristics of high-context and low-context cultures.

2. Invite participants to list on the chalkboard (or flip chart) the main characteristics of high- and low-context cultures. After this is done, pass out Handout 2: Analytical vs. Intuitive Thinking, which is a summary of these two approaches or "ways of reading the map." Then synthesize the two lists.

3. Read through the list of situations identified in Handout 3: Daily Tasks, and quickly check each one "Low" or "High" according to whether you personally feel you would respond intuitively (high-context) or analytically (low-context) to that situation.

4. Now go back over the list of situations, and for each one invite both high- and low-context participants to tell what they might do in each situation.

5. Debrief the group. You may want to conclude with something like this:

   A. You will probably have noticed by now that it really is possible to approach almost any problem either analytically or intuitively, but that the resulting behavior will be very different, depending on which approach you choose.

      Example: Getting yourself from your office to another place in town.

      High-Context (intuitive):

      Refusing to establish any criteria or conditions beforehand and taking whatever means of transport happens to turn up; heading out and just "following your nose."

      Low-Context (analytical):

      Listing alternative courses of action open to you (i.e., car, train, bus, foot, plane), establishing criteria for selecting a course of action in light of your objective, selecting the course of action which best meets these criteria, and implementing it.

   B. Other tentative conclusions that the group may draw to which you may wish to add some of your own:

      ○ It seems that we can only identify and work with formal and informal aspects of culture, using an intuitive, high-context approach.

      ○ A low-context approach seems more appropriate for technical aspects of culture.

      ○ Cultures in which a high-context approach is common tend to be societies bound by tradition and extensive formal rules (e.g., China, Japan).

      ○ For cultures in which a high-context approach is common, innovation is associated with technical behavior that does not violate formal rules (e.g., technological innovation in Japan, Hong Kong, Korea, Singapore).

      ○ One paradox is that for cultures in which a low-context approach is common, innovation is associated with high-context, intuitive approaches that escape the constraints of existing technology.

Further Reading

Burgoyne, John, and Roger Stuart. *Management Development: Context and Strategies.* Farnborough, England: Gower, 1978.

de Bono, Edward. *The Use of Lateral Thinking.* New York: Penguin, 1971.

Kepner, C. H., and B. B. Trogoe. *The Rational Manager.* New York: McGraw-Hill, 1965.

Moore, P. G., and H. Thomas. *The Anatomy of Decisions.* New York: Penguin Modern Management, 1976.

Pedler, Mike, and Tom Boydell. *Management Self-Development: Concepts and Practices.* Farnborough, England: Gower, 1981.

This activity was inspired by Edward T. Hall's *Beyond Culture.* New York: Doubleday/Anchor, 1977.

Handout 1: High- and Low-Context Cultures

Let us use a "map" metaphor for a moment. Imagine that a certain traveler constantly refers to the map as a means of orientation while another traveler prefers to keep the map in his or her head only as a general idea rather than a detailed record of every feature in the terrain. Of this second traveler, we say that he or she prefers to work intuitively, using hunch or feel and relying on sense of direction.

This second traveler makes the first traveler feel uneasy. "How does this intuitive person know he or she is on the right track?" the first traveler will ask. The first traveler needs specific evidence or indicators, needs to check with the map to get clear directions. To him or her, the intuitive person seems to work almost by magic, and that feels risky.

We call this first traveler analytical, using facts and figures and relying on spoken language and past experience (the map is, after all, a distillation of other peoples' experience) in order to move about.

The contrast illustrated here is fundamental in some human psychological paradigms. It is the contrast between the thinking and feeling dimensions of Carl Jung's psychological types. It is the contrast between the modes of operation of the "adult" and "little professor" ego states in transactional analysis. It is the contrast between the left and the right hemispheres of the human brain as identified by R. Ornstein and others.

The different modes of thinking exhibited by the two travelers is prevalent among human cultures, and this can be seen in their use of language. Anthropologist Edward T. Hall calls this contrast in the cultural sphere that between low-context (LC) and high-context (HC) cultures.

In *Beyond Culture,* Hall (1977) describes the contrast as follows:

> A high-context (HC) communication or message is one in which most of the information is either in the physical context or internalized in the person, while very little is in the coded, explicit, transmitted part of the message. A low-context (LC) communication is just the opposite: i.e., the mass of information is vested in the explicit code. Twins who have grown up together can and do communicate more economically (HC) than two lawyers in a courtroom during a trial (LC), a mathematician programming a computer, two politicians drafting legislation, two administrators writing a regulation, or a child trying to explain to his mother why he got into a fight.

> Although no culture exists exclusively at one end of the scale, some are high while others are low. American culture, while not at the bottom, is towards the lower end of the scale. We [Americans] are still considerably above the German-Swiss, the Germans, and the Scandinavians in the amount of contexting needed in everyday life. While complex, multi-institutional cultures (those that are technologically advanced) might be thought of as inevitably LC, this is not always true. China, the possessor of a great and complex culture, is on the high-context end of the scale (91).

A high-context communicator is thus sensitive to situational or contextual data, what we would describe as information that is implicit in the situation, and requires relatively little content or explicit information in order to understand what is going on.

A low-context communicator is highly sensitive to standardized data from which he or she can generalize and requires a large amount of content, or explicit information, in order to understand what is going on.

The intuitive, "feely" traveler who keeps the map in his or her head is high-context, while the analytical, "factual" one who has it constantly in hand is low-context.

The activity which follows makes the assumption that our psychological type is partly innate and partly learned: each of us engages in both intuitive and analytical processes many times each day, but for reasons that are partly cultural (i.e., learned), partly innate, and partly situational, we tend to have preferences for one approach rather than another.

Handout 2: Analytical vs. Intuitive Thinking

Analytical
- Relies on prior knowledge and experience
- Deductive (or inductive)
- Mind is in control
- Collects data in light of prior knowledge and experience
- Appropriate where circumstances are predictable and familiar
- Planning/theory-oriented
- Explicit (i.e., verbal)
- Rational
- Content-oriented (low-context)
- Linear
- Concerned with patterns of events
- Sensitive to causality (i.e., events related to each other over time)

Intuitive
- Relies on immediate sense data of the moment
- Intuitive
- Mind is not in control
- Regards data collecting as an objective in itself
- Appropriate where circumstances are upredictable and unfamiliar
- Action/event-oriented
- Implicit (i.e., nonverbal)
- Nonrational
- Context-oriented (high-context)
- Holistic (big picture)
- Concerned with "shape" of events
- Sensitive to synchronicity (i.e., events occurring together)

Handout 3: Daily Tasks

a. Getting yourself from an office to another location in town
b. Finding out who is married to whom at a party
c. Determining the mood of a meeting
d. Finding out where to catch the bus and when
e. Identifying people's professions
f. Deciding when it is time to leave a dinner party
g. Deciding how many people are in favor of a resolution
h. Deciding on the right moment to ask for a raise in salary
i. Picking winning numbers in a lottery
j. Identifying a market need for a product
k. Identifying people's state of health
l. Deciding how much time is needed in getting to the airport
m. Knowing what your partner is thinking at a given moment
n. Preparing the annual budget
o. Finding out train times at the station

Intercultural Self-Disclosure Scale

Donald W. Klopf

Objectives

1. To make explicit the proposition that how much of yourself you reveal to others is a function of *whom* you are talking to and *what* you are talking about (assuming the conversation is private).
2. To become aware of the need to develop strategies to handle situations where the other person expects you to be more forthcoming than you want to be (i.e., in cultures with different concepts of public and private space).

Participants

Any number of adolescents or adults.

Materials

Pens/pencils, handout.

Setting

Anywhere participants can write and then discuss in small groups, followed by whole-group discussion.

Time

45 minutes (10 minutes for filling out scale, 20 minutes for small-group discussion, 15 minutes for debriefing whole group).

Rationale

Revealing intimate information about oneself, called self-disclosure, plays an important role in developing close relationships. It concerns messages about the self that listeners would not likely acquire unless the speaker were to disclose it personally. The disclosed unmasks the self as he or she perceives the self. Disclosure increases along with intimacy in the relationships and when disclosure is rewarded. It increases also when a person has a need to reduce uncertainty in a relationship.

Self-disclosure is a universal phenomenon, but it differs from culture to culture in perceived intent, amount, depth, positiveness, and honesty. Euro-Americans disclose about a wider range of topics than Japanese do. Ghanaians disclose readily about family matters, whereas Americans disclose more about career concerns. Euro-Americans disclose more than African Americans, Mexican Americans, British, French, Germans, Puerto Ricans, and Japanese. East Asians differ from Americans in what they think should be revealed and what should be kept private. Americans are more inclined to self-disclose to a wider range of people than Japanese and Koreans, and Koreans are more willing to disclose themselves to a wider range of people than Japanese.

Proven to be a reliable and valid research instrument, the Self-Disclosure Scale (handout) has been repeatedly used in cross-cultural studies. The results confirm that self-disclosure differs from culture to culture in terms of fifteen topics commonly talked about in interpersonal interactions. For example, in a study comparing Japanese, Korean, and American respondents to the scale, the findings indicate the majority of the respondents from the three countries will willingly self-disclose about their preferences in television programming, motion pictures, automobiles, and the like with any of the target persons, except that Japanese and Koreans will not so disclose to different-culture strangers. The majority from the three countries will disclose to their lover or best friend on any of the fifteen topics. Japanese and Koreans are reluctant to talk with their fathers about their feelings regarding sex, face and body, abortion, and pornography while Americans will avoid discussing only sex matters with their fathers. Mothers will be confided in regarding all topics by Americans. Politics, abortion, and pornography will not be discussed by Koreans with their mothers, while the Japanese avoid talking about pornography with the mother. On all topics, Americans are more inclined to self-disclose to more target persons, including cultural strangers, than Japanese and Koreans.

More effective communication results from self-disclosure, from revealing more of a person's hidden feelings. This usually occurs more readily in dyadic relationships than in small-group conversations or public speaking situations. The more people there are, the harder it becomes for the speaker to judge how accepting people are of him or her. A speaker is more inclined to bare his or her soul to one person than to many, and certainly not with strangers. The better we know someone, the more willing we are to self-disclose.

Interestingly, classroom exercises in self-disclosure tend to be failures because those taking part are reluctant to share their true selves with others, a normal reaction in the classroom. We allow some people to know certain things about ourselves and others to know other things. We do not share everything with everyone.

Underlying the self-disclosure process is a key principle: Our interaction with another person will be more effective and efficient when we know more about the other person and the other person knows more about us. Considering what to reveal, we should reveal information that will enhance the communication, information unknown to the other person, and information the other will not learn from our friends or family.

What to self-disclose? The fifteen topics offer clues as to what we can share with others. But before self-disclosing on personal topics such as those, we should be in a proper setting—a nonthreatening situation, one free of rejection or disapproval—a setting of goodwill.

Procedure

1. Introduce the Self-Disclosure Scale (handout). How much of yourself do you disclose to people? What innermost thoughts and feelings do you reveal, to what degree, and to whom? This exercise asks you to examine what you would disclose to potential communicative partners mother-father, lover-friend, and stranger-acquaintance, from the culture you are studying. The exercise asks you to identify the topics about which you would self-disclose and what level of self-disclosure you would reach on each. The levels are:

    0 = would not disclose any of my thoughts or feelings on this topic

    1 = would talk in general terms about this topic

    2 = would disclose fully on this topic

    3 = would lie or misrepresent my thoughts or feelings on this topic

    Distribute the handout and instruct participants to place the appropriate symbol in the space provided for each topic and for each partner on the Self-Disclosure Scale therein.

2. Invite participants to join a small group (3-6 people). Select one or a few items on your Self-Disclosure Scale to share with the other members of your group. Everyone is free to make whatever comments or questions he or she wants.

3. Reconvene participants into one large group. Facilitator leads in an exploration of:

    a. How did you feel about your own self-disclosure scale? Any surprises?

    b. What items did you select to share with the members of your small group? What items did you purposely avoid sharing?

    c. How did you feel about the small-group session? What did you discover?

    d. How do you handle situations where the person you are talking to wants you to disclose more than you want to?

    e. Have you experienced talking to someone from a different culture where the other person's sense of what was a proper question differed from your own? (If no one can think of any examples, the facilitator provides some. Example: Saudi Arabian man asks stranger how much he earns.)

    f. How would you deal with questions that appear to you to be very personal but which are commonly asked in another culture?

Further Reading

Barnlund, Dean. *Public and Private Self in Japan and the United States.* Yarmouth, ME: Intercultural Press, 1989.

Condon, John C., and M. Saito, eds. *Intercultural Encounters with Japan: Communication-Contact and Conflict.* Tokyo: Simul Press, 1974.

Klopf, Donald W. *Intercultural Encounters: The Fundamentals of Intercultural Communication.* 3d ed. Englewood, CO: Morton, 1995.

Klopf, Donald W., and Myung-seok Park. *Korean Communicative Behavior: Recent Research Findings.* Seoul: WCA-Korea Press, 1994.

Klopf, Donald W., and Ronald E. Cambra. *Personal and Public Speaking.* 5th ed. Englewood, CO: Morton, 1995.

This activity appears in Donald W. Klopf, *Workbook for Intercultural Encounters.* Englewood, CO: Morton, 1995.

Handout: Self-Disclosure Scale

0 = would not disclose   1 = would generally disclose   2 = would fully disclose   3 = would lie

Topic	Mother	Father	Lover	Friend	Different-Culture Acquaintance	Different-Culture Stranger
1. My face and body	_____	_____	_____	_____	_____	_____
2. Diseases, injuries I have	_____	_____	_____	_____	_____	_____
3. My personality	_____	_____	_____	_____	_____	_____
4. Sexual relations	_____	_____	_____	_____	_____	_____
5. Amount of money I have	_____	_____	_____	_____	_____	_____
6. Financial problems	_____	_____	_____	_____	_____	_____
7. Work/school problems	_____	_____	_____	_____	_____	_____
8. My occupational goals	_____	_____	_____	_____	_____	_____
9. My views on politics	_____	_____	_____	_____	_____	_____
10. My views on abortion	_____	_____	_____	_____	_____	_____
11. My views on pornography	_____	_____	_____	_____	_____	_____
12. My feelings toward this person	_____	_____	_____	_____	_____	_____
13. My likes and dislikes in TV, cars, films, sports, etc.	_____	_____	_____	_____	_____	_____
14. My family background	_____	_____	_____	_____	_____	_____
15. My girl-/boyfriends	_____	_____	_____	_____	_____	_____

The Magic Box:
Exploring Stereotypes

Jorge Cherbosque

Objectives

1. To demonstrate the role that stereotyping plays both at work and in our personal lives.
2. To show one way that stereotypes can be broken.

Participants

This game should be played with a minimum of 4 and a maximum of 20 people. (With more than 20 people you can divide the group into several small groups playing simultaneously.)

Materials

8 x 10 index cards
pencils
masking tape
a box (metal or cardboard)
a bottle
a newsprint flip chart

Time

30 minutes of playing, 45-90 minutes for debriefing.

Setting

A room large enough for participants to walk around and visit with one another.

Theory

Stereotypes have traditionally been a destructive force in human relations and in the lives of many of us as individuals. This exercise is designed to transform the stereotyping process into a dialogue which will make us more aware of our tendency to stereotype others and will prepare us to become more effective, efficient, and humane in our coping with diversity in our jobs and in our lives.

Researchers and practitioners have studied the development and function of stereotypes, concluding that using them is a way we cope with the uncertainty of the world and attempt to make life more predictable. Yet they have also been the cause of a great deal of pain and suffering. In being stereotyped, people become victims of narrow judgments and prejudice which prevent them from advancing in our society. This experiential activity attempts to address the issues of the different stereotypes we are subjected to and the ways they influence our lives both at work and in our communities.

Many excellent studies have been conducted which give insight into the role of stereotyping and the influence stereotypes have, especially as self-fulfilling prophecies. This exercise is based on Gordon Allport's ideas about how to create awareness of stereotypes and how to break them. Allport believed that in order to break stereotypes the following three conditions must be met:

1. Bring people into a situation in which they enjoy equal status.
2. Create a climate of interdependence.
3. Arrange for personal contact in which people can appreciate their uniquenesses as well as their similarities.

"The Magic Box" follows Allport's suggestions in all three areas.

Procedure

1. The facilitator asks people in the room to make a circle and then, one by one, to introduce themselves briefly. It is important to develop a sense of group cohesion so that members feel safe and so that an environment of openness and disclosure develops. The facilitator explains the goals of the activity and posts them on newsprint.

2. Explaining that we all have multiple identities, the facilitator asks each participant to choose an identity, one that is important to that person's sense of self. Some chosen by previous players have been: white, black, working mother, homosexual, heterosexual, psychologist, short man, housewife, bald man, cancer patient, executive, middle manager, union member, accountant, lawyer, Jew. It is very important that people choose an identity they feel strongly about.

3. Participants are asked to write their chosen identity on an 8 x 10 card. Then, using masking tape, they tape the card to their bodies. When finished, members circulate around the room so that people become aware of the diversity which exists among them.

4. The facilitator asks players to think of a stereotype associated with their identity. It should be a stereotype that has caused them some personal pain. Once people come up with a stereotype, they write it on another 8 x 10 card, which they keep. Examples of stereotypes which people have previously chosen are:

    Jews are materialistic.

    Latinos are lazy.

Short men are unattractive and wimpy.

Housewives are unintelligent.

Blacks are good dancers.

Germans are cold and aloof.

5. The facilitator gathers the group in a circle and places a bottle on its side in the center and then says that he or she will spin the bottle and that the person at whom the bottle is pointing when it stops is expected to talk about his or her stereotype: What is bothersome about it? What kind of suffering has it caused? How does the person feel about it? What effect has it had both in and outside the workplace? In some groups, spinning the bottle may be unacceptable. If so, the facilitator asks for people to volunteer and take turns.

6. The facilitator allows each person to talk for several minutes about his or her stereotype. As each participant finishes talking, the facilitator asks the group if they know someone who in him- or herself negates the stereotype. It is not enough to say that they have heard about someone. They need to have had *direct contact* with someone who disproves the stereotype. If someone in the group has had such contact he or she is asked to describe the person and make clear how the stereotype is negated by him or her.

> Example: It is not enough to say, "My uncle told me he knows a Polish man who is intelligent." It is correct only if we say, "I have a friend named Josh who is Polish. We met in college. He's very intelligent. He was able to help me understand Kierkegaard's concepts. Without him I don't think I could have passed that class."

7. If someone in the group is able to demystify and disprove the stereotype, the individual who "owns" it takes the 8 x 10 card on which it is written and puts it into the "magic box" in the center of the group. If no one among the participants has known someone directly who negated the stereotype, or if one only knew people who *fit* the stereotype, the individual with the stereotype can't get rid of it and must, instead, attach the card to his or her body with masking tape.

8. Play continues until all group members have had the chance to talk about their stereotypes and either get rid of them or attach the card to their bodies.

Debriefing

It is very important to spend ample time debriefing this exercise. Some leading questions to help begin are:

a. How did you feel about this game?

b. How did you feel about getting rid of your stereotype?

c. How did you feel about attaching your stereotype to yourself?

d. What are the functions of stereotypes?

e. How can stereotypes be broken?

f. How have stereotypes played a role in your workplace, organization, or otherwise; and how can they be neutralized?

Who Should Facilitate This Activity

Experience has shown that members disclose very personal and sensitive information and that the pain and anger of being stereotyped emerge. Therefore, it is important that only a person trained in interpersonal communication and skilled and experienced in cross-cultural training should conduct this simulation. If you don't have the training skills and experience, or if you feel uncomfortable with trainees expressing feelings of pain and anger, this simulation exercise may not be the right one for you to use.

Further Reading

Allport, Gordon. *The Nature of Prejudice*. Reading, MA: Addison-Wesley, 1954.

Brislin, Richard. *Cross-Cultural Encounters: Face-to-Face Interaction*. Elmsford, NY: Pergamon, 1981.

Miller, N., and M. B. Brewer, eds. *Groups in Contact: The Psychology of Desegregation*. Orlando, FL: Academic Press, 1984.

9

Describing Cultures through Their Proverbs

Sandra Tjitendero

Objective

To explore cultural assumptions and values by examining proverbs, since they usually express values and attitudes broadly accepted and understood within a culture group.

Participants

Any group.

Materials

Paper, pencil, and list of proverbs.

Setting

No special requirements.

Time

Variable.

Background

Although we all know a proverb when we hear one, it is difficult to define the term precisely. One of the best definitions is: a short, pithy, epigrammatic statement which sets forth a general, well-known truth. When viewed as part of a communicative act, they are vehicles for sending messages about the values, norms, and customs of a people. They serve as witnesses to the social, political, ethical, and religious patterns of thinking and behaving of a culture group.

Proverbs are characterized by a touch of the fanciful in their unique turn of phase, unusual use of a word, or perhaps a specific rhythm. Many are paradoxical, or antithetical, while others are strongly metaphorical. In the educational setting, we are concerned with how to use proverbs to get at underlying cultural assumptions. We can examine proverbs for their exaggeration of attitudes commonly held by a cultural group. Hyperbole, personification, and alliteration are common attributes of proverbs which give us an unforgettable phrase or kernel of thought. Each proverbial statement has a quality of permanence in the culture and recurs in its folklore.

Procedure

1. Give participants a sheet of paper containing the following proverbs:
   a. "You got eyes to see and wisdom not to see."
   b. "Muddy roads call the milepost a liar."
   c. "Every bell ain't a dinner bell."
   d. "A mule can tote so much goodness in his face that he don't have none left for his hind legs."
   e. "The graveyard is the cheapest boardinghouse."

2. For each of the above proverbs, choose a phrase from your own culture in your own language or dialect which approximates the meaning of the proverb. Use familiar words and symbols; for example, "Kumquats are both sweet and sour." (If you aren't familiar or comfortable with "kumquats," substitute "oranges.")

   What does the original proverb mean? What is its message?

   What does the proverb indicate to you about the culture? Can you generalize about it, whether it is traditional, rural, submissive, dominant, happy-go-lucky, cautious, etc.?

   What are the dominant values of the culture represented in the proverb?

3. If you can, think of some proverbs you are familiar with which convey a similar message. If you cannot, why not? For example, "For the turtle to make progress, it must stick its neck out" is similar to "To learn to swim, you must first get your toes wet." The message is similar, the symbols are slightly different.

4. Try to identify the culture from which the five examples above are drawn. Say what type of culture you think it is, and some reasons why you characterize it that way. Elaborate.

   At the end of the exercise, the trainer reveals that the culture we are looking at is Afro-American slave—these are real examples of proverbs taken from the folk literature.

   The first example points to the ability of the slaves to accurately perceive what goes on around them, but the sense not to "see" or acknowledge that reality. Emphasis is placed on not knowing something which would get you into trouble if you acknowledge being aware of it.

   In the next example, the muddy roads are relatively impassable, therefore the person traveling them cannot count on the mileposts to gauge how long his or her journey will take. We can tell this is a rural culture and that its people are used to translating signals into their own particular knowledge about dealing with nature.

The third example indicates frequent conflicts between the dinner bell, a safe cue, and the bell calling slaves in from the fields, sometimes a warning of imminent danger. Again, the rural culture is reflected in the image of the bell.

The mule often looks as if he will be a helpful farm animal, but his legs still can kick you or refuse to budge—so don't be deceived by appearances. Again, an agricultural culture is reflected in the imagery; there is a realism born of knowing the environment and what you can expect.

The graveyard, in the last example, is escape from the troubles of a hard life—so don't worry about death—death is a kind of freedom for the slave, rest from all the hard times.

This activity originally appeared in Margaret D. Pusch, ed. *Multicultural Education: A Cross-Cultural Training Approach*. Yarmouth, ME: Intercultural Press, 1979.

10

U.S. Proverbs and Core Values*

L. Robert Kohls

Objective

To use proverbs as a springboard to an analysis of core values.

Participants

Any group interested in U.S. culture (can also be used to analyze proverbs of other cultures).

Materials

Flip chart (or chalkboard), markers (or chalk).

Setting

No special requirements.

Time

45 minutes.

Rationale

Although proverbs or axioms are not nearly so popular in the United States as they were a century ago, everyone carries in his or her head several dozen familiar examples. Benjamin Franklin single-handedly created quite a number of them for us.

Because of their overfamiliarity and even old-fashioned tone, we often think these "old chestnuts" surely have no application to our life today. Yet it is amazing to see what an accurate indicator of twentieth-century American values they still are.

---

*Versions of this exercise have appeared in at least two other collections. The editor felt nevertheless that it was such a perfect companion piece to Ms. Tjitendero's that it should be included here as well.

One of the hidden points of this simple exercise is that any single fragment of our culture is a microcosm of the whole. All we have to do is stop and notice it and take the trouble to analyze it, which, as you will see, is an easy enough task.

Procedure

1. The trainer begins by writing a couple of traditional American proverbs on the flip chart. Because of their current political *in*correctness, I often purposely choose to start with these two:

   "Little children should be seen and not heard."

   "A woman's place is in the home."

   Precisely because they are controversial, they catch the group's attention, and the trainer can make the point that, indeed, they are absolutely *inapplicable* to our modern world—along with the point that, aside from a few exceptions such as these, the staying power of *most* of last century's proverbs show great staying power and have remained surprisingly current.

2. The trainer asks each trainee to jot down five or six proverbs he or she is familiar with. This produces more examples than can possibly be used in the exercise, but expedites the process of collecting examples orally in the next step.

   Note: Trainees who are not from the United States can be invited first to share proverbs from their own cultures. If the guests are from Western European countries, the Americans will be surprised to find that their proverbs—British, German, or whatever—are often variations of what we thought of exclusively as our own, which, of course, highlights the European origin of mainstream American culture. If the trainees are from cultures very different from those of the West, the exercise will be enriched by the different perspectives introduced by their proverbs. To illustrate this point, here are two proverbs from Ethiopia:

   "Never, never catch a lion by the tail. But if you *do*: Never let go!"

   "A farmer with his grapes planted too close to the roadside and a man with a too beautiful wife—both of them will have the same problem."

3. Ask the trainees to call out the proverbs they have written down. The trainer selects those he or she wishes to use and writes them out on the left half of the flip chart. The list includes a dozen or so.

4. Then the group, under the guidance of the trainer, analyzes each proverb to see what one or two "core values" or meanings each contains. These are recorded on the right half of the flip chart.

Examples of Proverbs:	**Core Value(s)**
Cleanliness is next to godliness.	Cleanliness
Time is money.	Value of time (frugality)
A penny saved is a penny earned.	Thriftiness
Birds of a feather flock together.	Guilt by association (preference for the culturally similar)
Don't cry over spilt milk.	Practicality
Waste not; want not.	Frugality
Early to bed, early to rise, makes a man healthy, wealthy, and wise.	Diligence
God helps those who help themselves.	Initiative
It's not whether you win or lose, but how you play the game that counts.	Sportsmanship
A man's home is his castle.	Privacy (private property)
No rest for the weary.	Work ethic
You've made your bed, now sleep in it.	Responsibility for wrongdoing (getting what you deserve)

5. Discuss each value with the trainees (1) to explore its meaning as fully as possible and (2) to assess the degree to which it still governs the behavior of Americans. Are the values represented those solely or primarily of Americans in the cultural mainstream or of minority groups as well?

   Start with a paramount value not illustrated by one of the proverbs listed (e.g., belief in God, success, all human beings are created equal, competition is good) and see if anyone can recall a proverb that fits it—or, if not, see if anyone can make up one that does.

An earlier version of this activity appeared in Margaret D. Pusch, ed. *Multicultural Education: A Cross-Cultural Training Approach*. Yarmouth, ME: Intercultural Press, 1979.

Section III: Courting the Intercultural Perspective (activities 11–19)

Introduction

The beginning of wisdom is the ability to see at least two sides of a story.

The Emperor's Pot, developed by Donald Batchelder, is a venerable approach to simulating contact between two hypothetical and very different cultures and acquainting participants with diverse worldviews. In terms of the emotional shock of self-discovery, *The Emperor's Pot* may not be as successful as *BaFá BaFá*, but it does have the strength of providing an enjoyable vehicle for experiencing to a limited extent the contrasts between disparate societies. Nineteen dimensions of culture are incorporated into this model of East and West cultures and the debriefing on these dimensions justifies the two hours spent on the simulation.

Indrei Ratiu suggests a private, introspective way for an individual to become conscious of the feelings of disorientation that inevitably accompany a sojourn in a strange setting. The individual visits for a few hours a location within his or her larger community where some subcultural feature makes it alien to his or her experience.

Anne B. Pedersen provides a three-phase methodology for, respectively, distinguishing statements of fact from statements of inference, identifying personal perspectives on yourself and others, and developing "double-loop" thinking—understanding what the other person thinks of your behavior. The setting for developing these three skills is an altercation between roommates who have very different culturally influenced styles.

Films can provide rich material for discussing cultural norms. Linda B. Catlin and Thomas F. White developed a training session based on an analysis (they use the term "deconstruction") of the movie *To Kill a Mockingbird*, a film whose age makes it "new" to most contemporary students.

Ann Hubbard takes another source as grist for her cross-cultural mill—survey statistics on the values of American and French youth. The survey data are presented in a pleasingly graphic way. The facilitator helps the large group identify the most frequently mentioned items, paying attention to both central tendencies and variability. The survey results for French youth are then distributed and studied.

Donald W. Klopf, in "Word Meanings across Cultures," explores how cultural differences can affect the "meaning set" people associate with words such as "education," "family," and "marriage." While this originally appeared in print as a cognitively styled learning unit, the editor adapted it to fit the format of an experientially styled activity. The major difference between the two learning styles is that in the former, principles are learned and from these the meaning of data is deduced. In the latter (experiential style), data are manipulated to induce principles. Cognitive-style learning has the advantage of taking less time to absorb; experiential-style learning takes longer but stays longer.

Judith M. Blohm designed "How We Each See It: Host Parents" for debriefing host families in Youth for Understanding student exchange programs. It gives host parents a chance to express their views on the experience. "Likes," "dislikes," and "don't understands" are probed in an orderly process. Hosts are helped to see the cultural basis for many adjustment problems and—importantly—to understand that these difficulties can be resolved. This approach can be used to defuse conflict whenever the cleavages form along cultural lines—"race," ethnicity, gender, social class, and age.

We develop selective perception at an early age, and it sometimes prevents us from seeing the cross-cultural richness of our own communities. Donna L. Goldstein contributes "The Cooperative Map Exercise" to encourage participants to make this discovery. Individuals draw a map of their community, highlighting things that may be of interest to a foreign visitor. Participants are then put in small groups to draw a composite map. The catch is, they can include on the map only places they have visited personally. A secondary objective of this activity is to show participants an advantage in working together (you "see" more). The activity also can be used with multiethnic work groups. (The activities in Section IV deal with working together as their primary objective.)

The last activity of this section was prepared by Judith M. Blohm and Michael C. Mercil, again for Youth for Understanding. It structures a panel discussion in which returnees talk about their overseas experience in a way useful for other students who may be interested in going abroad—a critical adventure in courting an intercultural perspective.

11

The Emperor's Pot

Donald Batchelder

Objectives

1. To simulate visiting a culture that differs from your own ("East" culture vs. "West").
2. To help the participant become aware of some dimensions of culture (e.g., time, history, work) and their impact on behavior.

Participants

16–50; requires two facilitators.

Materials

Handouts 1, 2, and 3; chalkboard and chalk or flip charts and markers; a large pot or urn.

Setting

Two rooms, one large enough to accommodate the whole group.

Time

1½ to 2 hours. Note: If time allows, a variation of the process is to stage the exercise before lunch or dinner, and break for the meal after the first negotiating and subsequent planning session, but *before* the final negotiation. Participants can stay in roles throughout the meal hour, continue discussions with the other side, and then plan and carry out the final negotiation.

Rationale

Simulation games and exercises have enjoyed a modest acceptance in recent years, their objectives ranging from getting in touch with one's psyche to reapportioning the world's resources. Those of us who have already shaken hands with our psyches and are interested in the use of simulations for cross-cultural training realize that the world's resources, in terms of useful simulations, are inequitably distributed. Most exercises are directed toward technical training, history, diplomacy, ecology, conflict resolution, public affairs, economic strategies, military tactics, and, lately, to values clarification. Only a few are designed specifically for cross-cultural orientation; we are resource poor or, in the jargon of the times, "less developed."

One of the reasons for this is in the nature of cross-cultural training itself; it is an impressionistic, thought-provoking enterprise which does not lend itself readily to Western game theory. Most of the games we play are designed in a competitive mode. A participant or team tries to outwit, defeat, or outguess the other side. The spirit of competition is regarded as a healthy value in our society; presumably it is, but cross-cultural understanding operates on a different plane, and winning or losing has little relationship to it.

I wanted a simulation which would enable the group to participate in a culturally authentic exercise immediately, without lengthy briefings or the complex preparations which render many simulations cumbersome. My intent was to work out a pattern that enabled everyone to be involved at an acceptable level without forcing anyone into discomfort, to plan something combining seriousness with a bit of fun (since many exercises are devoid of fun), and, finally, to design an activity which could be managed by no more than two staff members and accommodate as many as fifty people. I decided to build the exercise around my 1,600-year-old Silla Dynasty burial urn from Korea and called it "The Emperor's Pot."

I set up two cultures, East and West (the simulation is sometimes referred to as the "East-West game"). I discarded details like gross national product, population figures, growth rates, and mineral resources. Instead, I concentrated on basic cultural values of a Confucian society and a Western society. A set of cultural values and a description of their respective purposes was available for each side. I designed possible roles for each side with titles only. Development of actual roles was left for each participant to work out during the exercise with the help of the values lists, a set of brief instructions, and a small amount of coaching from staff. The purpose was for participants to get away from the usual fixation on facts and information, use their imaginations to work themselves into suitable role portrayals, and devise enough structure to make it work.

Briefly the scenario is this: The urn has great spiritual significance for the East. According to legend, it appeared during a time of famine, brimming with rice, and saved everyone from starvation. Because of this, the urn is beyond price. The West has heard about the urn and wants it for its oriental collection. A series of planning sessions and bilateral discussions take place, culminating in a joint session between the two large groups; the whole is followed by analysis and discussion.

Procedure

1. Divide participants into two groups, East and West. Assign each group to a separate room. (A facilitator is present in each room.) Provide the West group with Handout 1: The West; the East group with Handout 2: The East. The facilitator helps each group understand its assigned culture and develop behavioral strategies. (30-40 minutes.)

2. A delegation from each group visits the other group. (Each visit about 5 minutes; this phase lasts about 40 minutes.)

3. After the visitor exchanges, each group assesses what happened.

   The West team generally starts out in a competitive mode, being Western, and dedicates itself to designing strategies to acquire the urn. They are usually frustrated by the spirituality of the East, the long cyclical view of time, and the East's apparent indifference to material blandishments of the West. Often, at some point in the process, the West decides to shift goals and take time to get to know the culture of the East; the acquisition of the urn then becomes secondary. The West teams occasionally remain in a competitive win-lose mode and pursue acquisition of the urn to the end of the simulation—and even afterward. In either case, this competitive trait becomes a focus for discussion after the exercise ends, along with other elements of culture, behavior, and sensitivity.

4. Both groups are called together in the larger room. Facilitators ask the West group to describe the culture of the East group, writing the points on the chalkboard or flip chart. Then the East group is asked to describe the culture of the West. In each case the group being described remains silent. (10 minutes.)

5. The East group then reacts to the list of culture traits the West put together of Eastern culture and describes, for the benefit of the West group, their culture. The West follows the same procedure, setting the East straight about Western cultural norms. (10 minutes.)

6. Facilitator debriefs participants. What do you think of the descriptions of the two cultures? How realistic are the values? (Are there cultures with values like these?) How reasonable are these values? How did you feel while interacting with the visitors from the other culture? (What were your gut reactions?) What did you learn from this activity? (20–30 minutes.)

At first the debriefing discussion can become fixated at surface levels—what is wrong with the simulation, etc. This is normal, but brush it aside gently and explain that a simulation is nothing more than a simulation, unless you take it deeper and examine what can be learned from the process. All simulations have flaws and limitations, and leaders should not allow the discussion to become snagged on a critique of the elements of the game.

The West will want to know, for example, if the West side has ever obtained the Pot. The answer is no—and they have been trying since 1973. The West often thinks it has been dealt a stacked deck. This leads nicely into a discussion of the whole purpose of the exercise. All of our Western games tend to be dedicated to the obliteration of the other side, amassing all the chips, *winning*. The West, in this game, often goes to great efforts and persuasion to try to win by obtaining the Pot—but would they really win if they got it? Some West groups decide among themselves partway through the process that perhaps obtaining actual possession of the Pot is secondary—that they should get to know and understand the other culture first, get acquainted with its people, and try to establish communication and friendship.

Get both sides to think about the ways in which they approached their roles, how they approached the other side, and what they may have experienced or learned as a result. You might also ask them how they might revise their approaches if they had another chance to go through the exercise.

Ask the West group how and in what ways and why they might have changed their tactics and thinking after their first exposure to the East group. Turn this around and ask the East the same thing. The West usually feels somewhat powerless.

The West participants often point to their instruction sheets and cite the statements which specifically tell them to get the Emperor's Pot. They also use such phraseology as "money is no problem" (or is it?), and "every man has his price" (or does he?). These items can be useful in the discussion because they center on Western beliefs and values and enable you to raise the question of whether or not the West group ever considered shifting goals, forgetting about obtaining the Emperor's Pot, and perhaps simply trying to get to know the East.

The East groups, despite their poverty and spirituality (as opposed to power and technology), often frustrate the West as they begin to see that their system of indirect answers, never saying no directly, and so on, provides them with a level of subtle power. To what extent did the East consciously frustrate the West by using the power? To what extent did they take conscious steps to educate the West and to make them more comfortable? In doing one or the other, did they remain true to their listed cultural values and behaviors?

East groups often deal defensively with outsiders and strangers, which is normal behavior for people from the Secluded Kingdom. Ask West and East about this issue of defensiveness, suspiciousness of strangers, etc.

How can you overcome the frustration of trying to communicate, make the other side understand, come to some mutual basis for agreement? What were the communication issues involved? What process can you develop in order to approach another culture sensitively? To what extent must you, can you, did you play a role in order to make culture contact work? What do you feel about your willingness to play a modest role in order to communicate, make yourself acceptable, get along?

Handout 1: The West

Instructions

- Your group represents an authentic Western culture. You are rich and powerful.

- Recently, your government has had several exchanges of diplomatic correspondence with the Secluded Kingdom, a traditional Eastern society which has lived in isolation for centuries.

- The Emperor's Pot is in the possession of the East. It is a most valuable part of their ancient cultural heritage. It is an artifact with mythical significance, and although they are a poor country by Western standards, they will be reluctant to give it up. However, you have been assigned the task by your national museum, with strong urging from your government itself, to obtain the Emperor's Pot for your country's oriental collection. Money is no problem.

- You will be engaging in discussions and negotiations with representatives of the Secluded Kingdom. In plain terms, your group has been formed to obtain the Pot, at whatever cost, although tact and diplomacy may not allow you to come right out and state this directly during negotiations. It is important for you and your Western colleagues to develop a set of tactics or approaches which may help you to achieve your objective.

- Although the people of the Secluded Kingdom are isolated and poor, they are intelligent and are known by others in their region of the world to be shrewd traders. They are reported to be a spiritual people, lacking in materialism, but your government is convinced that agreements can be reached for, as we all know, every man has his price.

- Culturally, it is important for you to figure out which approaches might be acceptable to the other side in order to smooth out the path to your objective, which is the Emperor's Pot. At the same time, you should try to stay within the outlines of the value system defined for you in the attached information sheet.

- Typically, you tend to be hardworking, pragmatic, success-oriented, and efficient; you plan ahead and try to use time productively.

- Your first task during the thirty-minute planning period is to read yourself into your role, study the cultural and behavioral clues, and decide two main issues:

  1. How many delegates, and which ones, should you send to the East to talk with their representatives; what should you talk about; what approaches should be used?

  2. Who will remain in the West to receive the visiting delegation from the East; how should you set up the room to receive them; how do you stage an appropriate meeting with them; what approaches and lines of discussion should you follow?

○ After the thirty-minute planning period, you will be instructed to send your team of delegates to the East; at the same time the East will send its team of delegates to you. Both your traveling delegation and those who host the delegates from the East should make careful observations on the values, attitudes, and behaviors of the East. You will be able to share these observations with one another during a second planning session directly after the first exchange of visits and prior to the final negotiating period. The notes and observations made in the first negotiation period will enable you to make informed guesses and assumptions about productive ways to deal with the East during the final negotiation period.

○ The basic schedule is as follows:

Phase I	Planning Period	30 minutes	In the West
Phase II	First Negotiation	15 minutes	Both sides exchange delegates
Phase III	Planning Period	20 minutes	In the West
Phase IV	Final Negotiation	15 minutes	Neutral territory. All participants in same room
Phase V	Discussion Period		

○ A staff person will be in the room during your planning periods to help with questions and to assist with the exchanges of delegations.

○ Below is a list of the different Western roles.

Roles:

International Business Manager/Holiday Inn hotel chain
Curator of National Museum (expert on oriental art)
Protocol Officer
Representative of Tourism Industry
Agriculture Specialist
Cultural Anthropologist
Public Relations Man or Woman
Confucian Scholar
Diplomatic Officer
Professor of Asian Studies
Collector of Oriental Art
Intelligence Agent posing as an area studies specialist
Journalist
Chief of your Task Group (forceful administrator)
Recorder—to list all values, characteristics, etc., of the other side
Timekeeper—to keep each phase of exercise exactly on schedule
GOD (Group Organizational Director)—the overall organizer of the West team

West—Cultural Traits and Values

(these will govern your role behavior)
"I"—Egocentrism

Individualism—Self-reliance, initiative expected from each. Status achieved by own efforts. Equal economic, social, political opportunity regarded as right of individual. Achievement is good and requires competitiveness.

Social Conformity—Outward conformity to opinions of others and to dressing "appropriately."

Activism—Being active, especially in face of uncertainty, is a virtue. Achievement and goal-oriented activities are important.

Pragmatism—Practical ingenuity applied to social as well as materialistic problems. What is good is what works.

Progress—Change in itself is good. Improvement, especially personal, is a duty.

Nature—Humans have the responsibility to control Nature.

Efficiency—Expected not only of machines but of social organizations and individuals as well.

Time—Precisely measured and must be used productively and efficiently.

History—Seen as a linear progression.

Aggressiveness—Ambition, competition, self-assertiveness to achieve success are emphasized. High status, once attained, does not confer right to treat the lower class as inferior. Excelling is good, but empty boasts or boasting about success are bad.

Freedom and Discipline—Preschool: discipline from parents. School age: increased freedom and responsibility. Adulthood: time of greatest freedom. Old age: considered less productive, less active, less capable, less free.

Mobility—Great physical and social mobility is good.

Work—Valued as an end in itself. Personal effort, energy output: good. Laziness: bad.

Money—An economic tool, plus yardstick for social status, influence, power, satisfaction.

Youth—Highly valued. Old people wish they were young again. Elders feel outmoded by rapid change.

Education—Means to an end, especially to attain skill, money, status. Affects family prestige.

Authority—Rules/laws generally obeyed, but don't like to be ordered to obey. Authorities must not infringe upon individual rights. Mild suspicion of authority.

Moral Superiority—A moral smugness stemming from conviction that the West's people are special, with a set of values and conditions that have made them unique.

Handout 2: The East

Instructions

- Your group represents an ancient Eastern culture, the Secluded Kingdom. You are poor but proud. After many years of isolation, you have begun an exchange of diplomatic correspondence with the West, and soon you will meet their representatives to discuss subjects of mutual interest. These brief instructions are designed to help you prepare for your first meetings with people from the West.

- The Emperor's Pot is in your possession. It dates back to A.D. 400. It is *the* national treasure, and culturally you cannot give it up under any circumstances. The West wants the Pot, and their representatives are under pressure to get it.

- It is in the nature of your culture to be very agreeable, to be very polite, to try always to answer affirmatively, whether you mean it or not. You will be talking and negotiating with Western delegates and must avoid blunt refusals and flat, negative statements. You are unable to tell their delegates that they will *never* obtain the Emperor's Pot. You may discuss it at length, agree (or seem to agree), and go along with their lines of inquiry and discussion, but there are deep reasons for not letting the pot go.

- For example, one legend about the Emperor's Pot tells how, in a time of famine, when hope seemed lost, the Pot appeared, brimming with rice, and fed everyone. Thus it has almost mythical value and is intertwined with the great spirituality of your people.

- Culturally, it is important for you to avoid strong, direct eye contact with the delegates from the West. You look them in the eye, but only momentarily.

- Typically, your delegates and spokesmen will practice the ancient art of dealing through a third party. Example: your Chief Spokesman will do *some* of the talking as a delegate to the West, or as host to the West delegation, but may defer often to other members of your group. If a Western delegate directs a difficult question to you, it is appropriate to give a partial response, then bow politely, and suggest that perhaps the Royal Astrologer could best answer the question. Your purpose is not to frustrate the West, but rather to remain true to your own ways. It is the task of the West to figure out how your culture operates.

- Your first assignment, as you begin your planning, is to read yourself into your role by studying the cultural and behavioral clues on the attached information sheet and to decide two main issues:
  1. How many delegates, and which ones, should be sent to the West to talk with their representatives; what should you talk about; what approaches should be used?
  2. Who will remain in the East to receive the visiting delegation from the West; how should you set up the room to receive them; how do you

stage an appropriate meeting with them; what approaches and lines of discussion should you follow? For example, you may want to receive the Western delegates by seating them on the floor, the earth being of great importance in your agricultural society. Or you may provide chairs for the visitors from the West while you sit on the floor.

○ After the thirty-minute planning period, you will be instructed to send your team of delegates to the West, and the West will send its team to visit you. Your traveling delegates, and those who remain at home to host the visitors from the West, should make careful observations on the values, attitudes, and behaviors of the West as they interact and talk with them. These observations will then be shared with one another during a second planning period after the first negotiation and prior to the final negotiation. Your insights into the West will enable you to refine your roles and prepare yourselves for the final negotiation.

○ The basic schedule is as follows:

Phase I	Planning Period	30 minutes	In the East
Phase II	First Negotiation	15 minutes	Both sides exchange delegates
Phase III	Planning Period	20 minutes	In the East
Phase IV	Final Negotiation	15 minutes	Neutral territory. All participants in same room
Phase V	Discussion Period		

○ A staff person will be in the room during your planning periods to help with questions and to assist with the exchanges of delegations.

○ The different Eastern roles are listed below. Your list of cultural values is at-tached.

Roles:

Chief Spokesman
Paramount Lady of the Kingdom
Minister of Education and Culture
Security Officer
Political Officer
Protocol Officer
Information Officer
Honored Linguist and Speaker of Tongues
Royal Astrologer
GOD (Group Organizational Director)—the overall organizer of the East Team
Most Honored Grandmother
Spokesman #2 (most honored)
Royal Guardian of Peace and Tranquillity
Royal Keeper of Sagacity and Wisdom

Spiritual Adviser of the Realm
Honored Historian of the Hermit Kingdom
Most Honored Guardian of Royal Antiquities
Cultivator of Rice for All Mankind
Minister of the Ocean Depths and All Creatures of the Sea
Professor of Western Civilization

East—Cultural Traits and Values

(these items will govern your role behavior)
"We"—Group orientation.

Overlapping Ego—Expectations/morality of community more important than that of the individual. Individual always in social role; cannot do anything to conflict with group.

Form—Outward form is of major importance. Manners extremely important. Must participate in activities considered important by group, even though one disagrees.

Passivism—Confucian idea of endurance is prevalent. Acceptance of fate, life, etc.

Pragmatism—Confucian or community morality is applied to social issues and problems.

Progress—Change is both negative and positive. Technical change may be necessary; social change is bad.

Nature—Nature is considered beautiful/good. Conformity to rule of nature considered good.

Efficiency—Considered less important than higher values such as form, face, conformity to custom.

Time—Not precisely measured, except in business/science. Time not a primary consideration. The present, not the future, is given utmost value.

History—History is seen as a cyclical phenomenon rather than a linear progression.

Humility—Related to social status. One never takes advantage of one's rank. One always defers to one of higher social rank and always appears humble. Persons of high rank must even make attempts to defer to and honor social inferiors.

Freedom and Discipline—Preschool: much freedom, little discipline. School age: discipline begins at home and with teachers at school. A function of the school system rather than the parents at this age. Adulthood: many responsibilities to family and community. Old age: great freedom, shown much respect, considered to have great wisdom.

Mobility—Important because one has duties to family and community.

Work—A means to an end rather than an end in itself. Has no value in itself.

Money—Saving for the sake of saving is seldom considered a virtue. "Face" is involved—i.e., spending an entire year's income for an elaborate wedding will increase family prestige. Price is regarded as an index of quality.

Age—Great reverence for age, which brings wisdom, authority, rich perspectives on life as well as certain privileges. One always uses honorific terms when addressing an elder.

Education—A source of discipline and a means of enhancing family prestige and status. Confucian idea of education to create the true gentleman. Women, historically, were not formally educated.

Authority—Confucian values stress caution and obedience to authority. Individual rights get little consideration. Vertically organized hierarchy regarded as most orderly and harmonious.

Moral Superiority—A moral smugness stemming from a conviction that the East's people possess a set of values and conditions that have made them unique.

Handout 3: Facilitators' Guide

The Emperor's Pot was designed as a cross-cultural simulation which can be started as soon as the participants are assembled, and can be mounted quickly and efficiently. Two staff are needed to manage it.

To begin: Assemble the participants in one room, hold up an old ceramic or clay urn of some kind, and announce that it is the Emperor's Pot. It has great spiritual significance for the people of the East (The Secluded Kingdom) for, once during a great famine, so the legend goes, when hope was all but lost, the Pot appeared, brimming with rice, and fed everyone. The West has heard about the urn and would like to acquire it for the outstanding collection of oriental art in their national museum.

Have participants count off by ones and twos around the room. Ones can be East and twos can be West. Have one side leave immediately for another room.

Next, hand out to each participant, East and West, in the separate rooms, a copy of the description of the exercise and the lists of values and behaviors for either East or West which are attached. Tell them to start reading the information sheets, while the staff member in each room hands out name tags to each person with a given role to be played. This is done arbitrarily, though participants generally accept the roles as given, and begin to think themselves into the roles as they read their instructions. They should have about thirty minutes to read, discuss, and plan. A variation which works well is to have one person read the instructions aloud. The East needs a bit of coaching by staff. They are spiritual people, never say no directly, defer to one another, etc. They are curious about the West, and their government leaders have exchanged diplomatic correspondence with the West after centuries of isolation, but meeting Westerners is a new experience for them.

For the first five or ten minutes, nothing seems to happen as the participants read the cultural clues and values lists. During this period you may begin to think you have a disaster on your hands, but don't panic. Soon the participants begin to sort out their thoughts, ask questions, discuss possible approaches, and organize themselves for participation. You may have to remind them that they have to select a team of delegates to visit the other side and arrange a reception and meeting with the visitors who come from the other side. If they have not done so themselves by the time twenty or twenty-five minutes have elapsed, you should suggest that the visiting delegates who will be going to the other side and the welcoming group which will host the visiting delegates should form separate groups to finalize their plans.

A visiting delegation of from five to eight people seems to work quite well.

It is helpful to point out to all participants at the outset that allowing themselves to succumb to silliness will ruin the simulation. It is an exercise to enjoy, but the intent is serious and there is an appropriate etiquette involved. Most groups have a good time with the simulation but take it quite seriously. A bit of humor and laughter may occur during negotiations, but fits of giggles and silly behavior are unacceptable.

The thirty-minute planning session is a preparation for a first exchange of visits. The East will send a delegation to the West, and at the same time the West will send a delegation to the East. One task for each side is to decide how many and who should constitute the delegation, what they should talk about, and how they should pursue their goals. The other task is to decide who should remain behind to receive the visitors, how to set up the room and receive them, and what to talk about. It is not necessary, but works well, to provide a thermos of iced tea and some small cups or glasses so the East can perform a tea ceremony for their Western visitors. Crackers and jelly can be offered by the Western hosts to their visitors from the East, or each member of the delegation can be given a flower.

Staff announces the time for the exchange of visits and coordinates things so that each group moves at the same time. The first set of visits should run for about fifteen minutes, after which they should be cut off. Delegations then return to their group, where they have a chance to compare notes with their colleagues and get ready for the final negotiation.

The final negotiation takes place presumably in some neutral territory, a third room or larger hall if you have one, or in one of the rooms that you have been using. During this final phase, move all participants into the room so that all can hear and take part in the discussion. Each side may designate specific spokespersons to carry the negotiating responsibility, but groups can be arranged in a way which allows everyone to participate. This final session can be stopped after about fifteen minutes, although groups which get deeply involved in the simulation often wish to carry it on for thirty minutes or more, staying in their roles and continuing the negotiations. If this occurs, by all means let the session continue, but terminate it when it is clear they have reached an impasse.

At the conclusion of this final negotiating session, the facilitator or coordinator should keep everyone in the same room and announce that it is time for a discussion of the simulation. Some points for discussion are appended, but perhaps a few additional explanatory notes might be useful in the management of the simulation itself.

The roles listed for East and West are titles only. It is the responsibility of each participant to imagine him- or herself into the assigned role. While this seems to be a tall order at first glance, participants ranging in age from thirteen to sixty-five have managed to do it quite well. One of the pleasures of the process is the apparent endless variety of good characterizations which participants are able to invent. The one role on each side to which specific responsibility is assigned is that of Group Organizational Director, who should take initiative in the planning, with help from staff if needed, to steer participants in positive directions, to get decisions made, and to keep the process moving on schedule. The other roles are left to the participants' imagination. As stated, once the two teams are in their separate rooms, roles are generally handed out arbitrarily on name tags. A variation is to read off the roles aloud and ask participants to select the roles they prefer. (Hand print titles on 4 x 6 file cards.)

Staff Notes for the East

After the East participants have read through their instructions and cultural clues, they often decide on a slowdown strategy in their interactions with the West. This is acceptable up to a point, for they have a different view of time than the West, but it is helpful to point out to them in planning sessions that their purpose is, after all, to get to know the West, to be good hosts and polite visitors, and to be true to their own thoughtful, courteous, gentle nature. Thus, they can prepare a ceremony for the West delegates to share their excellent tea and to honor their guests, but should not tie up the entire period with one ceremony.

East teams occasionally decide to rigorously avoid any discussion of the Emperor's Pot. Actually, it is more true to their cultural values to talk about it, to explain its significance to the West, if the West asks about it, and to share information about it in the context of its meaning for the Secluded Kingdom. The East does not have to "get tough" with the West in any sense. The slow, spiritual, gentle unfolding of conversation and events is tough enough for the West delegates, who are usually in a hurry.

It is sometimes helpful if you suggest to the East team the appropriateness of telling the West how honored the East is to have such an opportunity to meet them and how much they are looking forward to other meetings in the future. This first, tentative opening up of face-to-face relations with the West is, after all, a major step.

The West frequently offers foreign aid, tourism, advanced technology, agricultural assistance, and other things in exchange for the Emperor's Pot. The East is generally interested in such offers, but not to the extent of disrupting the harmonious balance of humanity, nature, spirit, and culture. It is important for the East to discuss such offers graciously, keeping in mind that the West may have more than a little trouble understanding how a poor nation can resist their blandishments, as well as considerable difficulty understanding the East's spiritual approach to life.

While it is not necessary, a few odds and ends of costumes, if readily at hand, add a touch for the East players.

Staff Notes for the West

In some ways, the West roles are more difficult than those of the East, perhaps because they look familiar, and everyone tends to read the United States into the description. This is acceptable, but staff should encourage them to read the cultural clues and instructions carefully because there are specific ideas and suggestions which emerge from the reading. At times, West participants seem reluctant to take on leadership roles right away, so you as a staff person may have to encourage them slightly. For example, the participant who has a specific role assignment which requires leadership and initiative may feel uncomfortable and be reluctant to act or speak up at first. Thus, the one who has a specific role assigned may not wish to plunge directly into it. When this happens, swapping roles is perfectly acceptable and is often done among West teams in the first planning session. This helps to get the process moving.

West teams often mill around for a while looking for a strategy, then fix upon a specific plan of action, perhaps getting stuck with a course of action without really examining possible alternatives. A few suggestions from staff on other approaches, or staff help in getting other ideas heard, can be helpful. For example, West teams often start thinking in terms of stealing the Emperor's Pot, or resorting to violence by kidnapping someone from the East. There must be other alternatives worth exploring. Sometimes it helps to have someone read the instructions aloud to the whole West team, after they have had a few moments to go over them individually.

As participants think about their roles in the West, they sometimes say, "I don't know anything about agriculture" or "What do I know about running a museum?" Encourage them to reread the values checklist and the directions, and get them to try to create the role by making it up and making it work. Their tendency toward literal-mindedness can be one of the elements of the discussion after the simulation. Another remark often heard in relation to an assigned role is, "I wouldn't be that way." Again, they should be encouraged to invent the role and make it work.

It is preferable if the staff member assigned to help the West encourages and coaches gently without assuming a total leadership role. If a participant who is strong-willed and persuasive has everyone on a negative or unproductive course of action during planning sessions, it is appropriate to step in and ask for alternative suggestions, but in general it is best to let them work out their own approaches and plans without giving too much of the story away.

Tips for Trainers

I have conducted the exercise several times each year and have been fascinated to observe the inventiveness, imagination, effort, and serious cultural learning that is stimulated by it in each new group. It has gone badly on two occasions, but there was a compensating gain each time. Once a staff member dissolved into laughter during sensitive negotiations, breaking an otherwise serious mood; students rallied to the other side, trying to make up for the outburst, and discussed the matter at length later. On another occasion, the usually passive Eastern team turned militant and forced the West delegates to prostrate themselves on the floor while speaking to the East, a disconcerting breach of cultural guidelines. The West went along with it, and there followed a thoughtful discussion of meanings, motives, and feelings.

The purpose of *The Emperor's Pot* is a shared experience leading to a discussion of the whole process of approaching another culture and the cultural learning and skills which need consideration. It encourages participants to try different roles and social forms and can be used in preparation for work or study abroad irrespective of the East-West focus.

12

Simulating Culture Shock

Indrei Ratiu

Objective

To experience and observe your reactions to the not-OK feelings of disorientation in a strange cultural environment.

Rationale

This activity is based on two widely recognized premises:

1. that culture shock is endemic; we cannot inoculate ourselves against it, but we can *improve* our recovery mechanisms, and
2. that not-OK feelings, once recognized, have a tendency to disappear.

One of the most striking features of the state of disorientation we refer to as culture shock is that, like habitual drunkenness, we tend to deny its existence at the time. It is almost as if our Western industrial civilization denies us the right to feel bad or disoriented: the only feelings that are OK are good feelings, feelings of being oriented and in control.

Participants

Any number of individuals.

Materials

Each participant needs a notebook and pencil.

Setting

Nearby location that is strange to participants, perhaps an ethnic enclave.

Time

At least 4 hours.

Procedure

1. Within your present cultural environment (country, town, etc.) select a particular location which seems especially "foreign" to you, and plan a visit to it. (Depending on the location you choose, access may be more or less difficult, and hence a greater or lesser degree of planning may be required.) The location must meet only three conditions:

   a. Your stay should be for at least four hours, i.e., a morning, afternoon or evening.

   b. You should be able to be a participant-observer within the location you choose. Do not arrange a "guided tour," observing "from the outside." Attempt to involve yourself directly in the *activities* of your chosen milieu.

   c. You must keep a record (notebook) of your experiences, thoughts, and feelings in the "foreign" environment.

   ### For example:

   Depending on your present situation, the location and activity you choose might be one of the following:

   - assisting the nurses in a mental hospital,
   - visiting a gay night club or other gay gathering place (if you are heterosexual),
   - participating in an unfamiliar religious ceremony,
   - visiting a nearby small town and interviewing the inhabitants about life there, or
   - spending an evening with an unfamiliar ethnic group.

   There are many, many possibilities. The critical element is to choose something *very* different from what you are used to and which causes—even as you think about it—some sensation of discomfort.

2. As you consider possible locations and begin to plan, write down your immediate feelings about doing the exercise and about the setting you have chosen. Watch for such reactions as:

   - I wouldn't go *there*!
   - What a stupid exercise!
   - What would I *do* there?

   Such reactions also count as feelings—feelings of dislike and irritation—and can tell you a lot about how you respond to unfamiliar environments.

3. Make the visit.

4. Even as you do it, observe yourself as you go. Make notes on your internal experience, on what you think and feel as well as what you do.

For example:

If there is a part of you that feels frightened, but another part that says: "How stupid to be frightened of such and such, it is only *x* miles from home" (or "These people are not all that different from me"), then write down "denied I was frightened."

This act of denial tells you a lot about your reactions to unfamiliar situations.

5. When you interrupt or end the experiment, recall when exactly you did so, what the cues for ending it were, what your feelings were at the time and afterward.

For example:

"Just sat and waited out my allotted time" could be an important indication of how you respond in such situations, as could: "Intensive experience; glad it's over; sad too."

6. When you have completed your record, find an article or a book that describes someone else's experience in another culture, especially someone who experienced and was able to describe something akin to culture shock. Are there ways in which your experience compared with that person's?

7. Consider comparing your experience—and your notes—with a fellow student or colleague. The learning will be deepened and intensified.

The first time you participate in the exercise you may deny that anything happened at all and simply be relieved that you have stopped wasting time and can now get back to normal. But isn't that in itself a significant piece of information about how you cope with unfamiliar environments? It is not uncommon to find a person in the throes of culture shock vociferously denying the obvious.

The intent of this exercise, of course, is to provide you with a small dose of "culture shock." It will not inoculate you against the experience when you go abroad, but it should reduce the surprises. The next step is to develop coping mechanisms geared to your particular mindset and personal needs.

13

Double-Loop Thinking: Seeing Two Perspectives

Anne B. Pedersen

Objective

To analyze a cross-cultural encounter from at least two perspectives, that is, from the viewpoints of *both* those involved.

Participants

1-30.

Materials

Handouts, paper and pencil/flip chart or chalkboard.

Setting

No special requirements.

Time

50-70 minutes.

Rationale

The incident provided below describes a cross-cultural encounter between two students, one the participant identifies with and the second, "the other."

The situation is examined first from "your" perspective and then from the perspective of "the other," with a distinction being made between the facts of the encounter and the inferences about it made by each. What you learn during this exercise is a way to see the incident, your role in it, and the values governing your behavior more accurately from the perspective of the other person.

Procedure

Note that this exercise was originally designed to be self-instructional. There are at least three ways to administer it:

1. Provide both the Incident and Analysis Handouts to participants, let them work on the exercise alone, and then share and discuss their reactions in small groups and/or as a whole group.

2. Ask participants to read only the Incident Handout. Then lead a discussion (based on the Analysis Handout) in which, with the help of a flip chart or chalk-board, you analyze the incident with them in the framework of double-loop thinking as discussed in the exercise.

3. Do the same as in #2, but provide the participants with the Analysis Handout to aid them in following the discussion.

Incident Handout

To begin, it is important to describe a conflict situation as completely as possible. Ilse has volunteered her problem.

You, Ilse, of German descent, and Leilani, from Hawaii, are first-year students at Chandler Engineering College. Both of you had requested single rooms in the college dormitory. However, because of unavailability, you were assigned as roommates.

From the start, the relationship seemed less than amicable. You created rules to divide ownership of the living space into equal parts. Your share was orderly and tidy. Leilani, on the other hand, stapled and taped colorful posters helter-skelter on the plaster wall, played rock music Polynesian style, and chatted with her island friends sprawled three or four deep on her bed, which normally could not be seen anyway due to clothes, clutter, and debris.

One morning after you left for class, Leilani remembered an important essay was due. She needed a dictionary for the task and took one from your shelf, without permission. As the day was warm, she gathered up her materials and left the dorm to write in the sun on the lawn. Joined by friends on the blanket, the dictionary was soon lost among the pile of multiple texts.

You returned shortly thereafter to find the wide empty space on the bookshelf.

During the blowup that followed, Leilani responded:

> I needed the dictionary just then. Books are to be used, not just looked at. Do you expect them to be ornaments? You are stingy, mean, obsessed; you value control over everything. Well, you won't control me. Someday, you'll find friends are more important than books.

You, Ilse, replied:

> The dictionary is mine. I spend my money on books not junk music, like you, and I take care of them. If you had a dictionary, you wouldn't know where it was. You are totally irresponsible. In your crowd, everyone just helps themselves. No respect for other people. And you abuse my books too. All you value is friendships. Well, you don't have mine. Good fences make good friendships.

Analysis Handout

A. This handout constitutes a guide to the application of double-loop thinking to the Ilse/Leilani incident. In analyzing the incident we ask you to take the role of Ilse.

B. *Objective Behaviors.* Note which statements in the incident are statements of fact, i.e., which refer to observable behavior. Make a list of specific behaviors for both yourself (Ilse) and Leilani. This list may look like the following:

Specific Behaviors

Ilse (yourself)	Leilani
1. requested a single room	1. requested a single room
2. created rules	2. stapled and taped wall posters to plaster
3. careful with possessions	3. played rock music Polynesian style
4. left for class	4. cluttered up her bed
5. returned to find her dictionary missing	5. took Ilse's dictionary and left dorm

C. *Inferences.* It is also important to note which statements are inferences, i.e., judgments made or conclusions drawn based on what happened. These commonly involve such things as expectations, values, and/or attributions of causality between events. Make a list of inferences found in your problem description. The list might look like the following (you can add others if you wish):

Inferences

Leilani infers that Ilse (yourself)	Ilse infers that Leilani
1. is stingy, mean, and obsessed with rules	1. is irresponsible and careless of possessions
2. expects books to be ornaments	2. is disrespectful of others
3. overvalues control	3. abuses Ilse's books
4. undervalues friendship	4. overvalues friendships

D. *Your Personal Perspective of Yourself.* An analysis of the encounter within a consistent framework will make your task easier. Below is a simple matrix to help you order your information.

My Personal Perspective of

Behavior	Expectation	Value
Myself		
Leilani		

To complete this matrix you need an accurate assessment of your own values and expectations as they influenced your behavior in the interaction. (This personal perspective of your behavior may look like the following.)

My Personal Perspective of Myself

Behavior	Expectation	Value
create rules, careful with books	to know where my books are	orderliness and responsibility

E. *Your Personal Perspective of the Other (Leilani).* Following the procedure outlined in D, above, begin an inventory of the values and expectations that may support the behavior of the other person. Your initial list of inference phrases will prove helpful in generating alternative interpretations. Choose the most likely one. The resulting sequence is *your personal perspective of Leilani's behavior.* This is a process of inference. Your conclusion may be confirmed or refuted through further communication and/or repeated observation. It might look like the following:

My Personal Perspective of Leilani

Behavior	Expectation	Value
takes my dictionary without asking	will abuse the property of others	orderliness and responsibility

F. *Your Personal Perspective of Someone You Know from a Different Culture.* At some point in the not-too-distant past, you will likely have interacted with a person who behaved differently from yourself in a cross-cultural encounter. Exercise your analytical skill by graphing the interaction from *your* perspective on the model below.

My Personal Perspective of

Behavior	Expectation	Value
Myself		
Different other		

G. *"Double-Loop" Thinking.* A more advanced stage in describing a cross-cultural event involves what is known as double-loop thinking, that is, knowing and understanding what the other person thinks of your behavior, expectations, and values. In simpler terms, it is called *taking the perspective of the other*. It is a relatively complex and difficult skill to master, involving patience, considerateness, time, and a certain tolerance for ambiguity.

Taking the perspective of another builds upon the assessment of the situation from your perspective. In other words, it is a further step away from perceiving the reality of the situation solely *as you see it*.

Staying with the same example of differing treatment of personal property, taking the perspective of another may be graphed in the following way:

Taking the Perspective of Another (Leilani)

Behavior	Expectation	Value
creates rules careful with books	to hoard information and property	control, possessions more important than people

This analysis necessarily involves a conjecture based on inference. As in making analyses from your personal perspective, this hypothesis must be checked (preferably with the other) to be confirmed or discarded. Making successive approximations closer and closer to what is accurate is the central ingredient of effective perspective taking.

H. *Practicing Double-Loop Thinking.* Here are a number of ways.

1. Continue to experiment with (and graph) taking Leilani's perspective, using the other inferences listed above, e.g., about friendship. Develop more inferences.

2. Assume Leilani's role and take (and graph) her perspective on Ilse.

3. Use the incident that you chose to describe in item F above relative to your personal perspective on a different other. Generate a number of alternative interpretations that the other person could plausibly draw about you. Choose the most likely and graph.

Taking the Perspective of a Different Other

Behavior	Expectation	Value

The other's perspective of me

In short, an accurate description of a cross-cultural encounter involves identification of your own perspective and, further, taking the perspective of the other.
In summary, the steps to follow are:

1. Describe the situation.
2. Objectively list the behaviors of both participants (don't use adjectives).
3. List statements of inference.
4. Relate the behaviors to the underlying expectations and values from your perspective. (Use the suggested matrix.)
5. Attempt to understand the other's thinking about *your* behavior, expectations, and values, i.e., take another's perspective. (Use the suggested matrix.)
6. Expand "taking the other's perspective" to an encounter you have had with someone from a different culture. Confirm or reject your understanding through further communication and/or repeated observation.
7. Learn double-loop thinking.
8. Practice double-loop thinking.
   I. *The final step*, of course, is to (a) assess the accuracy of your perspective on the other's perception of you and (b) explore ways in which you can modify your behavior to stimulate in the other an even more accurate (and more positive as well) perception.

Make a list and discuss with others who are doing this exercise effective ways to pursue these goals. Note: One of the simplest is to take the step suggested in item G above: check and/or confirm directly your perspective with the different other.

14

Cultural Deconstruction Exercise

Linda B. Catlin and Thomas F. White

Objective

Participants are encouraged to step back from their viewpoint as insiders and to assume the perspective of one unfamiliar with American culture while viewing a film which incorporates some of the values, beliefs, behaviors, and customs that make up American culture and then explaining those elements to a non-American.

Materials

Film (or video) and the equipment to play it, flip chart or chalkboard.

Setting

This exercise can be used in a variety of college and university courses, including cultural anthropology, business anthropology, marketing, management, international business, sociology, and intercultural communication.

Foreign student advisers can also use this exercise to orient American students who are planning to participate in study abroad programs. Its realism and pertinence can be enhanced by combining American students and foreign students on campus; in this configuration, non-American students can be paired with American students in the discussions following the film.

It is also appropriate for intercultural training programs in a corporate setting. It can be used in preparing international managers for their assignments abroad and in training managers to be more aware of the cultural diversity which exists within American business operations.

Development and Testing of Materials

The material was developed by the authors for use in their cultural anthropology and marketing courses. Linda uses the exercise at the beginning of her anthropology course to introduce students to the concepts of ethnocentrism and of emic/etic perspectives, and to help students be more aware and appreciative of the differences among cultures that they encounter throughout the course. Tom uses the exercise in his consumer behavior class in conjunction with material on cultural differences as they relate to the global marketplace.

Time

This exercise works best in a three-hour session. Films (videos) average 1½ to 2 hours in length, leaving approximately one hour for introducing the exercise, conducting the pair discussions, and discussing the results as a group. An alternative to showing the film in class is to put it on reserve in the media center and require that students view the film by a given date, leaving only the pair discussions and group debriefing for class time. Another way to break up the time required for showing a two-hour film is to show the first half of the film at the end of one class session, and then show the second half at the beginning of the next class. This method allows more time for discussion and debriefing after the film. Students also can be encouraged to answer some of the questions posed at the beginning of the film during the time between viewing the two parts.

Rationale

Before attempting to understand another culture, it is beneficial to understand the elements of one's own. This is not an easy task for most people, and it is especially difficult for individuals who have never lived in another culture or traveled extensively. One way to isolate some of the values, beliefs, behaviors, and customs which constitute one's own culture is through the "deconstruction" of a film or book reflecting that culture. Many films and books fit this description; for simplicity of illustration, we will use the 1962 film *To Kill a Mockingbird* as an example for this exercise. We like this particular film because it is new to many students born after the mid-1960s, and they can more easily view it without contamination from previously formed opinions and ideas.

Students often have a hard time generalizing about American values and distancing themselves from their own culture. They have a tendency to identify their personal values rather than values held by a majority of people in the culture. One way to overcome this tendency is to ask students, as a group, to brainstorm American values related to work, personal relationships, the community, etc. After the group has come up with a list, ask them to vote for the ones they consider to be most important to and/or most representative of American culture. This list then serves as a basis for discussion of topics related to the film.

Observation about outcomes: A number of students have observed later in the semester or term that they now view films with a different perspective, i.e., they view them not just as entertainment but also as sources of information about the world around them.

Procedure

1. The instructor or facilitator frames the viewing of the film in the context of using its content to explain certain elements of American culture to a person from another country. As the students watch the film, ask them to identify the parts of the film which a non-American might find confusing or about which he or she would have questions. Tell them that after the film, they will use these

elements to explain American culture to someone who has been in the United States for a very short period of time.

2. Give students the handout, which is a list of questions about the film designed to serve as a guide for their viewing.

3. After viewing the film, divide the class into pairs or into groups of four students. Ask one (or two) person(s) in each group to assume the role of a foreigner in the United States and the other person to assume the role of an American friend. The foreigner(s) should ask the American(s) about those elements of the film which he or she does not understand. The American(s) will try to explain how these relate to American beliefs, history, family relationships, and the legal system, not just to the plot of the movie. Instruct each pair or group to list the questions and answers they discuss. Allow 30 minutes for these small-group discussions.

4. After the pairs (or groups of four) have completed the questions posed in the handout, ask individual students to describe some of the elements of American culture which they identified in their discussions. List these on a chalkboard or flip chart and ask the group to add other aspects of American culture which they did not observe in the film. Did they discover anything new about American culture that they were unaware of before?

5. As a follow-up exercise, instructors may want to show and process within this kind of deconstruction framework a foreign film which illustrates elements of some other culture. It would be especially valuable, for instance, to undertake this kind of analysis of a film from the target country or a study abroad or other kind of cross-cultural training program. Instructors would want to provide some background about the culture shown in the film and/or assign pertinent readings related to it before showing the film.

Further Reading

Althen, Gary. *American Ways: A Guide for Foreigners in the U.S.* Yarmouth, ME: Intercultural Press, 1988.

De Vita, Philip, and James Armstrong. *Distant Mirrors: America as a Foreign Culture.* Belmont, CA: Wadsworth, 1993.

Summerfield, Ellen. *Crossing Cultures through Film.* Yarmouth, ME: Intercultural Press, 1993.

This activity appears in Linda B. Catlin and Thomas F. White, *Instructor's Manual. International Business: Cultural Sourcebook and Case Studies.* Cincinnati: South-Western, 1994.

Handout

Questions to consider when viewing *To Kill a Mockingbird*:

1. Why did segregation exist? Who were its supporters and its opponents?
2. How often did (does) black and white violence occur? Did (does) it go both ways?
3. Why did Atticus, a white man, defend a black man in the segregated South? What typically American cultural belief(s) underlay his actions?
4. Who should have been punished: Tom Robinson, the rape victim, the father, or Atticus?
5. Why did the lynch mob leave the jail?
6. Describe the nature of the relationship between Atticus and his children. Is this a typical relationship between American parents and their children?
7. Do you think that Scout is a typical American girl?
8. How should Boo Radley have been cared for after his parents' death? Why do you think Boo Radley was allowed to live as a "hermit" after his parents' death? What does this convey about American citizens' relationship with their government?
9. Are people in small American towns typically unfriendly toward strangers? Toward blacks?

15

Hopes and Fears

Ann Hubbard

Objectives

1. To examine one's own values and see that they often change and vary and that one's friends do not have precisely the same values.

2. To examine, compare, and contrast "hopes and fears" of French and American youth, paying attention to the value differences, similarities, and overlapping responses and to the social significance of the contrasting responses.

Materials

Chalkboard and chalk, or flip chart and markers (or overhead transparency); Handout 1: Values and Handout 2: Hopes and Fears (*Les Espoirs et les Craintes*).

Time

Approximately 1 hour.

Background

This exercise was originally developed for a French language class. It can easily be readapted for that context, though the form in which it appears here is designed for broader application. It is particularly valuable for students, but may be used as well with other groups where cross-cultural values clarification is an appropriate goal.

Procedure

1. Give each participant a copy of Handout 1: Values, and ask them to choose the three values most important to them personally as individuals, and also the three they agree (as a group) are most characteristically American. Certainly not all Americans hold a single set of values, yet most people share a profound belief in certain ideals or life goals.

2. Have each small group identify for the whole group the values, both personal and American, they agreed upon. Write them on the board.

3. Have the participants draw a line down the center of a blank piece of paper and list their hopes on the left side and their fears on the right. Ask what they want to accomplish, or what they want to see happen in their lifetime, what is best for themselves and for the world, and what will help them get started on their "hopes." What they believe might hinder them from seeing these things happen are their "fears." (Examples: crime, war, hunger, disease, ecological disasters, economic crises.)

4. Discuss the lists they've made, asking for volunteers to name some or all of their hopes and fears. List them on the board (or on an overhead transparency). Discuss the results—which were most common, which the most serious, etc.

5. Distribute Handout 2 and ask the participants to study the hopes and fears (les espoirs et les craintes) of the French students. The hopes were derived from a poll (Mermet, 1988) of French students 13-17 years old and the fears from a group 18-25 years old, but serve effectively the purposes of this exercise.

Discussion Questions

o What are the similarities and differences between the hopes and fears of the French students and those of the Americans?

o Do some hopes or fears appear to be uniquely French or uniquely American? Which ones?

o Are there any listings which surprise you? Why?

o Gudykunst and Kim (1984) suggest that values are the "desired objectives or ends of social life." Do you think that the hopes listed by both the French and American students reflect the values they hold, respectively?

o What values *are* reflected in the "hopes" listed?

o Do they seem consistent with values considered to be predominant in each culture?

o Do the fears connect with or reflect the values in any way?

Information for the Teacher

In a study done on the personal aspirations of American youth (Easterlin and Crimmins, 1988), the following statistics were recorded. You might integrate some of this information into your class discussion and/or compare the hopes and fears of your class with it:

	1976	1986	1996 Estimate
Finding purpose and meaning in life	64%	58%	
Having lots of money	46%	62%	
Desiring to work in a large corporation	58%	74%	
Desiring to work in a social service organization	72%	60%	

	1976	1986	1996 Estimate
Having at least two cars	40%	62%	
Having a recreation vehicle	36%	51%	
Having a vacation home	29%	46%	
Having a new car every 2-3 years	28%	41%	
Giving my children better opportunities than I've had	50%	56%	

While these statistics relate mostly to material possessions and "success," they do exemplify the fact that values may change or be modified from generation to generation. It is important that students realize how dynamic some cultures are in this respect. It might be interesting and enjoyable to ask the participants to guess how the percentages might change in 1996 (third column) and compare estimates. (A caution: when dealing with public opinion percentages, be sure to interpret the results carefully, i.e., is a 50 percent response to a question significant?)

Bibliography

Easterlin, Richard A., and Eileen M. Crimmins. "Recent Social Trends: Changes in Personal Aspirations of American Youth." In *Sociology and Social Research* 72, no. 4, edited by Marcus Felson (July 1988).

Gallup, George. *The Gallup Poll.* Wilmington, DE: Scholarly Resources, Inc. This annual U.S. publication contains poll results revealing people's opinions on issues such as immigration, racism, crime, etc. While not focused uniquely on the opinion of youth, some polls involve young people and their attitudes, etc.

Gudykunst, W. M., and Y. Y. Kim. *Communicating with Strangers: An Approach to Intercultural Communication.* Reading, MA: Addison-Wesley, 1984.

Mermet, Gerard. *Francoscopie–Les Français: Qui sont-ils? Ou vont-ils?* Paris: Larousse, 1988. This book is published annually, compiling the results of various polls conducted in France on topics and issues such as values, health, the family, work, and society. (In French.)

Wood, Floris W., ed. *An American Profile–Opinionist Behavior.* Detroit, MI: Gale Research. This annual publication features opinion poll results on national issues, social habits, religion, family matters, and community in the United States.

Handout 1: Values

Examine the values listed below. Choose the three which are most important to you. (Mark the blanks with "me.") Do you think most people of your culture share those values? Why?

Work with two or three classmates to decide which three of the values listed are most likely to be shared by most Americans (write "Am." beside them) and explain why you think so.

Values:

_____ Beauty

_____ Harmony with nature

_____ Wisdom

_____ Close friendship

_____ Significant achievements

_____ Success

_____ Wealth

_____ Status

_____ Power

_____ Good health

_____ New experiences

_____ Change

_____ Individual independence

Handout 2: Hopes and Fears *(Les Espoirs et les Craintes)*

Hopes and Fears of French Students

Hopes *(Espoirs)*

Find an interesting profession (53%)
(Trouver un métier interessant)

Freedom (50%)
(La liberté)

Happiness in family (39%)
(Le bonheur familial)

Love (30%)
(L'amour)

Sports (27%)
(Le sport)

Travel (19%)
(Les voyages)

Music (15%)
(La musique)

Intellectual development (14%)
(Se développer intellectuellement)

Money (11%)
(L'argent)

Fears *(Craintes)*

Terrorism, violence (54%)
(Le terrorisme, la violence)

Economic crisis,
    unemployment (52%)
(La crise économique, le chômage)

Nuclear conflict (41%)
(Un conflit nucléaire)

World hunger (30%)
(La faim dans le monde)

AIDS (28%)
(Le sida)

Rise of dictators (22%)
(La monté des dictatures)

Ecological disasters (21%)
(Les catastrophes écologiques)

Decline of France (14%)
(Le déclin de la France)

Loss of national identity from
    immigration (13%)
*(La perte d'identité nationale, en raison
    du grand nombre d'immigrés)*

16

Word Meanings across Cultures

Donald W. Klopf

Objective

To disabuse participants of the notion that if we say something that makes good sense to us, it should make sense to everyone else. Or, to restate the point: To allow participants to see that words have different psychological meanings in different cultures.

Participants

Any number.

Materials

Paper, pencils/pens, flip chart and markers; chalkboard useful; Handouts 1 and 2.

Setting

Any place appropriate for both small- and large-group activity.

Time

Two meetings (separated by a few days). The first meeting (steps 1-7): 40 minutes. (Step 8 interviews are done out of class.) The second meeting (steps 9-12): 40-80 minutes, depending on the number of groups that need to report. Note: If the group is a large, culturally heterogeneous one (and therefore contains the diversity required for the step 8 interviews), this whole activity can be realized in a workshop day.

Rationale

Szalay and Fisher (1979) say that intercultural communicators must overcome "ego-centric bias" when speaking to someone of another culture. This bias involves the assumption that if we say something that makes good sense to us, it should make sense to everyone else. This notion, they say, is about as unrealistic as it is widespread.

One of the beliefs underlying the assumption pertains to the use of dictionaries. If we don't know what a word or phrase means, all we have to do is look it up in the dictionary. Unfortunately, dictionaries do not convey the entire subjective reaction elicited by a particular word or phrase. The dictionary meaning tends to be based on conventional and formal rules of use; it doesn't get at the psychological meaning attached to words. Dictionaries do not deal with the particular interests, perceptions, beliefs, and attitudes infused into words by culture.

Procedure

1. Facilitator asks participants to divide into small groups of five or six individuals. (If the participants know each other, this may bias the groups in the direction of same-thinking friends. This is all right; it will just highlight differences across groups.)

2. Explain that you are going to give them a word and that they are to make a list of things that they associate with that word, that is, things that the word means to them. Example: Take the word "rules." Some in the group may say that to them, "rules" means "helpful guidelines." Others may say it means "unwanted restrictions." Then the group participants are to agree among themselves which of those associations are (1) crucial, (2) very important, (3) important, or (4) not too important.

3. The facilitator gives participants the word "education," and allows them five minutes to develop a set of meanings and to rank them 1, 2, 3, or 4 in importance. (If necessary, the groups can be given more time to finish the assignment.)

4. One person from each group lists the meanings for "education" that were rated 1, 2, or 3 in a column on a flip chart, and the number of the ratings in a second column. Example:

sports	2
social life	1

5. Facilitator helps participants see the similarities and differences across groups.

6. Distribute Handout 1: The Priest and the Coach. Discuss the differences in how these two men view "education." Note that neither appears to include the idea of learning in his definition of education.

7. Assign a task to each small group. (1) Each group chooses the word "family" or the word "marriage." (2) Then each participant interviews two people, each from a different culture. One can be male and the other female, for instance. Or one can be from an English-speaking home and the other from a Spanish-speaking home. Or one can be a teenager and the other a senior citizen. Each group decides on what two cultures to include in its interviewing. That is, although one group may decide to interview Americans and French, and another group Tahitians and Maori, all the members of one group will be interviewing people representing the two cultures that their group selects. (3) The interviewer asks the subjects to say what the selected word means to them, and to then rank its

importance using the 1–4 point system they used with the word "education."

8. Participants conduct the interviews and meet with their small group to organize their findings. (It would be desirable to calculate the mean and standard deviation of each, if the group has a technically inclined participant.)

9. The whole group reassembles. Each small group reports its interview findings.

10. Facilitator helps group see the similarities and differences across all of the findings.

11. Distribute Handout 2: What "Family" and "Marriage" Mean in Selected Cultures. Facilitator leads a discussion of the findings as reported in Handout 2.

12. Facilitator leads discussion comparing the findings of the participant interviews and the findings of Handout 2. Major point to be made: There are both individual and group differences in what words mean. The meanings often diverge along cultural lines.

Further Reading/References

Osgood, Charles E., William H. May, and Murray S. Miron. *Cross-Cultural Universals of Affective Meaning.* Urbana, IL: University of Illinois Press, 1975.

Szalay, Lorand B., and Glen H. Fisher. "Communication Overseas." In *Toward Internationalism,* edited by E. S. Smith and L. F. Luce. Rowley, MA: Newbury House, 1979.

Takahara, N. "Semantic Concepts of 'Friendship,' 'Marriage,' 'Work,' and 'Foreigner' in the American, Japanese, and French Cultures." Reviewed in *Patterns of Communication in and out of Japan.* Tokyo: International Christian University, 1974.

Triandis, Harry C., et al. *The Analysis of Subjective Culture.* NY: Wiley-Interscience, 1972.

This activity appears in Donald W. Klopf, *Workbook for Intercultural Encounters.* Englewood, CO: Morton, 1995.

Handout 1: The Priest and the Coach

To illustrate that words have different psychological meanings, Szalay and Fisher take the word "education" and look at it from the frame of reference of a priest and a football coach, both individuals from the same culture. They pictured a set of meanings somewhat similar to those shown in this graph:

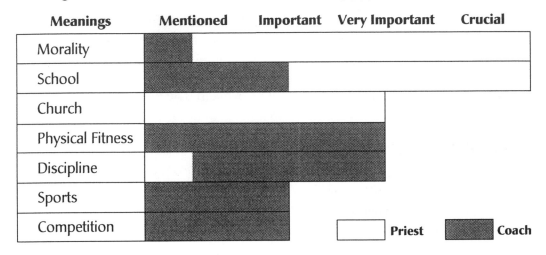

To read the graph, the unshaded portion represents the priest's interpretation of "education" and the shaded portion, the coach's. The length of each portion indicates the significance each person attached to the particular meanings. Thus, for the priest, "education" carries four possible meanings. "Morality" and "school" are crucial to an understanding of "education," "church" is very important, and "discipline" is mentionable.

The coach, obviously, has a different frame of reference regarding "education." To him, "physical fitness" and "discipline" are very important, "school," "sports," and "competition" are important interpretations, and "morality" is mentionable.

Based on what is known about their occupations, both priest and coach should have strong feelings about education. Yet, there isn't much agreement regarding its meaning between the two; they are coming from different frames of reference.

Handout 2:
What "Marriage" and "Family" Mean in Selected Cultures

Szalay and Fisher studied the meanings of words across cultures. From their study, Korean and American meanings for "family" were extracted and are listed by percent favoring each interpretation.

Family

Meanings	Percent of Respondents	
	USA	Korea
1. Children, brother, sister	19	25
2. Relatives	7	16
3. Happiness, fun	5	6
4. Family size, sex	0	5
5. Family support, livelihood	2	1
6. Activities, life	5	2
7. Togetherness, cooperation	6	3
8. Love, friendship	12	4
9. Home	11	6
10. Mother, father	30	29
11. Miscellaneous	3	3

A similar study was completed by N. Takahara across three cultures—American, Japanese, and French. From it, various interpretations of marriage were extracted and are listed on the next page.

Marriage

Meanings	Percent of Respondents		
	USA	Japan	France
1. Love	30	16	28
2. Respect	27	12	10
3. Responsibilities	24	15	8
4. Understanding	23	18	20
5. Helping each other	22	11	14
6. Problem sharing	22	17	13
7. Trust	21	27	17
8. Mutual encouragement	21	8	13
9. Interpersonal sensitivity	17	5	19
10. Accepting mutual freedom	17	10	16
11. Maturity	17	1	1
12. Family	17	20	9
13. Mutual fulfillment	16	6	18
14. Sex	14	11	22
15. Compromise	11	17	17
16. Passion	11	5	22
17. Children	13	16	7
18. United	9	6	15

17

How We Each See It: Host Parents
Judith M. Blohm

Objective

To help host parents express their feelings about their hosting experience and, with the aid of resource people, to help them look at creative ways of dealing with adjustment problems.

Materials

Blank flip chart paper; 3 x 5 cards; knowledgeable resource people.

Setting

Room with comfortable chairs large enough for host parents and resource people.

Time

1–1½ hours. Introduction (2 minutes), identifying feelings (15 minutes), discussing issues (60 minutes), conclusion (10 minutes).

Background/Rationale

Preferably held six to ten weeks after the foreign student has moved in with an American family, this activity for host parents in youth exchange programs comes when "the honeymoon is over" for many participants. Having trouble communicating may no longer be just embarrassing, it may be maddening or intimidating. The changes in family dynamics may be much more severe than initially expected. The misunderstandings from lack of really knowing each other may be extremely frustrating or even disruptive. One or the other party (or both) may have realized they had false expectations of the nature of this experience.

In this type of orientation, there are sessions when the family and the international visitor are together, and sessions when they meet separately. (There are parallel sessions for teens and children in the family, also.) The separate sessions, such as the one described here, provide each party the opportunity to share and discuss their frustrations with other participants like themselves and with special resource people. It is a constructive and balanced way to look at the experience *and* to work on the issues that are making it difficult. It provides them a way to share constructively their thoughts and feelings with their exchange students.

While this exercise is suggested for host parents in youth exchange programs, it is a viable and fruitful design for any group of people wrestling with problems arising out of close and continuous contact with people of different cultural backgrounds.

Procedure

1. Host parents assemble in a room by themselves, while their exchange student and children are meeting in parallel sessions elsewhere. The leader explains that this session will give host parents a chance to talk about the joys as well as the problems they have experienced in hosting an exchange student and will include the opportunity to seek advice on specific, particularly troublesome areas of concern. The final step will be to focus on how everyone can make the experience better.

2. The leader puts up three blank flip chart sheets and labels each with one of these headings: "Likes," "Dislikes," "Don't Understand." Participants are asked to assess their feelings and concerns about the hosting experience and then brainstorm them according to the categories identified on the three lists. Get as many thoughts and feelings as possible written on the lists without taking time to ask for clarification or discussion. There will be plenty of time for discussion later. The same ideas may appear on more than one list.

   Start with "Likes." Move on to "Dislikes" and finally to "Don't Understand." Some of the items that have been suggested in previous brainstorming sessions are:

Likes	Dislikes	Don't Understand
Anxiousness to please	Messy room or bathroom	So much time alone in room
Polite behavior		
Friendship with children	Doesn't get along with host children	How can he stand his hair (only washes it once a week)?
	Many phone calls received and/or made	Why doesn't she get more involved with her classmates, acquaintances?
	Poor language ability	

   When all lists are complete, ask if anyone has questions about any of the entries. Clarify for them and then summarize the exercise, and end by reminding them of the wisdom of emphasizing the things they like over that which puzzles or disturbs them.

3. Introduce *carefully selected resource people.* Have them form a panel in front or simply identify them where they are sitting (if a small group). Selection of resource people is critical. The ability of the person to deal with issues in a calm,

reassuring way while giving good concrete suggestions is extremely important. Former successful host families are often powerful role models and effective advisers. Exchange program staff and cross-cultural counselors also make good resource people for this kind of program. Pass out 3 x 5 cards to the host parents and ask them to write down any specific problems they have had or are concerned about that have not already been suggested during brainstorming. Collect the cards.

Ask the resource people to begin by addressing the items listed on the "Don't Understand" list. Encourage host families to add their ideas. Continue with items on the "Dislikes" list.

Finally, read the issues from the cards and discuss them.

Throughout this session, the leader should identify whom host families should contact for help, such as when a language problem continues to be severe, there are school problems, cultural adjustment problems don't seem to be working themselves out, student and host family have a major disagreement over important issues, etc.

In addition, where appropriate, supply information as to policies and procedures that the organization has that will help the host families resolve problems.

4. In the last few minutes of the session, the leader helps the host parents see that adjustment problems are normal and are solvable. Indeed, it is often in the solving of the problems that the greatest growth and learning take place.

Finally, the group decides how they wish to share the outcomes of the session with their exchange students when the latter join them. Here are some suggestions:
   a. One person may volunteer to summarize in his or her own words what happened in the session.
   b. Ideas may be grouped and presented according to (1) ways host parents can help exchange students, (2) ways exchange students can help host parents, and (3) what both need to do (such as communicate issues and problems, trust, get involved) to keep the relationship on an even keel and assure them all of a rich exchange experience.

Trainer Tips

The trainer of this session must have good facilitator skills and be able to work with participants who are angry or upset and who may reveal more about themselves and their feelings than they might wish. The trainer should have cross-cultural problem-solving skills.

This session will be enhanced if, both before and after it, parents and students engage in a mutually satisfying event together. An effective post-session activity is one in which parents and students work together to make plans for the remainder of the home stay.

Further Reading/Resources

Youth for Understanding Materials:

Blohm, Judith M. *Planning and Conducting Pre-Arrival Host Family Orientations.* Washington, DC: Youth for Understanding, 1987.

Educational and Training Services. *Host Family Handbook.* Washington, DC: Youth for Understanding, 1994.

———. *Passport to the USA: International Student Handbook.* Washington, DC: Youth for Understanding, 1994.

———. *Living in the USA Exchange Student Orientation Workbook.* Washington, DC: Youth for Understanding, 1995.

Other Youth Exchange Materials:

Grove, Cornelius. *Orientation Handbook for Youth Exchange Programs.* Yarmouth, ME: Intercultural Press, 1989.

Hansel, Bettina. *The Exchange Student Survival Kit.* Yarmouth, ME: Intercultural Press, 1993.

King, Nancy, and Ken Huff. *Host Family Survival Kit: A Guide for American Host Families.* Yarmouth, ME: Intercultural Press, 1985.

Family Communication and Relationships:

Satir, Virginia. *The New Peoplemaking.* Mountain View, CA: Science and Behavior Books, 1988.

American Cultural Values:

Althen, Gary. *American Ways: A Guide for Foreigners in the United States.* Yarmouth, ME: Intercultural Press, 1988.

Bennett, Milton J., and Edward C. Stewart. *American Cultural Patterns: A Cross-Cultural Perspective.* Yarmouth, ME: Intercultural Press, 1991.

This activity was prepared for this volume by Judith M. Blohm and appears in Judith M. Blohm and Michael C. Mercil, *Planning and Conducting Post-Arrival Orientations.* Washington, DC: Youth for Understanding, n.d. (circa 1985).

18

The Cooperative Map Exercise

Donna L. Goldstein

Objectives

1. To encourage individuals to explore further the cultural aspects of their communities.
2. To recognize the limitations of one person's frame of reference and experience.
3. To demonstrate the benefits of teamwork and cooperative learning.

Time

30 minutes to $1^1/_2$ hours.

Background and Trainers

This exercise was developed for a teacher-training course on multicultural education. Though most of my students lived in ethnically diverse communities, many rarely ventured out of their neighborhoods. When they did, it was to tourist sites or commercial districts. This activity has been very helpful at the start of a class or workshop to help motivate individuals to get to know each other better and to explore their communities.

After hearing about a Buddhist monastery in South Miami during this exercise, several Hispanic and African American students spent a wonderful afternoon there at the feet of a Thai Buddhist monk. At our next class they excitedly shared their experiences and insights. Later in the semester, a larger group from the class attended an Asian arts festival near the monastery and continued their investigation of Asian cultures.

If you use this exercise in a program in which there is more than one meeting, it is helpful to have students reflect on their initial independent map, and their group's map, in a journal or essay. Given time to reflect, many students were able to articulately describe their cultural isolation and commit to expanding their personal boundaries. These can be shared with the instructor in small groups or with the whole class.

Theoretical Framework

This activity graphically illustrates the concept of "synergy" (cooperation or interaction that generates more than the sum of the interacting elements), often described in literature on group behavior. It also is an effective demonstration of cooperative learning, where students work in small groups and share teaching and other roles and tasks. According to Johnson and Johnson (1984), cooperative learning groups promote positive interdependence and teach social skills and shared leadership. These types of learning experiences also develop more helping, encouraging, and assisting among students of varying ethnic backgrounds and abilities.

It has been useful in teacher training to use this activity to demonstrate the potential power and effectiveness of cooperative learning techniques. It is also helpful in discussing learning styles and Gardner's (1983) theory of multiple intelligences, as is demonstrated in the debriefing section.

The learning style implications of this exercise are also quite interesting. Using Gardner's seven types of intelligence, the following ways of teaching and learning are demonstrated:

o Linguistic learners absorb information best by saying, hearing, and seeing words. Their strong ability to memorize names and places makes them quite valuable to their group.

o Logical/mathematical learners excel at categorizing and classifying. They work well with numbers and will enjoy exploring the patterns and relationships of map making.

o Spatial learners learn best by visualizing and enjoy drawing and designing. They excel at puzzles, maps, and charts, and their maps will likely be the most accurate.

o Kinesthetic learners need to move and touch in order to learn effectively. This activity calls for two walks around the room, taping up their maps, and recalling times when they were physically in a certain place.

o Interpersonal learners require interaction and sharing with others. The cooperative aspects of this exercise promote interpersonal relationships both in and out of the classroom.

o Intrapersonal learners enjoy working alone on projects and pursuing their own interests. They would appreciate the individualized nature of the first phase of this activity.

Procedure

1. Instruct individual participants to draw a map of their city or county on a blank sheet of paper. On the map they are to note neighborhoods (and their demographic characteristics), cultural and historic sites, and anything which might be of interest to a foreign visitor. The notations may be made in any combination of words, pictures, or symbols. This should be done without consulting other classmates. The catch is that they must have visited each place personally for it to be placed on the map.

Example: In South Florida relatively few Anglos could give a visitor directions to the Haitian market. An even smaller percentage could say they have actually been shopping there. Only those in the latter group would be allowed to place the Haitian market on their map.

Choose an example from your city or county which may not be frequented by the majority of participants. (10–15 minutes.)

2. As participants complete their maps, post them with tape on the walls.

3. When all are posted, participants circulate to check out each other's maps.

4. After about 10 minutes the group convenes to discuss the experience thus far. Possible process questions include:

   a. Who would make the best tour guide? Why?

   b. Are there certain well-known places which do not appear on anyone's map?

   c. Are there differences that can be discerned by gender or ethnic background?

   d. Are the maps of longtime residents more detailed than those of newcomers?

   e. Who had difficulty with this exercise? Why?

   f. Who can easily see, draw, and utilize maps?

   g. Who has the "big picture" of their community? How can this be articulated?

5. Next, participants take their maps off the wall and form groups of 5–6 people. The groups then take 15–20 minutes to draw collective maps on large posters or pieces of flip-chart paper. Again, one member must have been to the place for it to be included on the collective map.

6. The collective maps are posted when completed, and participants again circulate and compare approaches.

7. The concluding discussion can emphasize any or all of the following:

   a. How does the greater detail on the collective maps stimulate greater synergy in the groups?

   b. Does the map exercise suggest what can be gained from exploring other cultures and lifestyles?

   c. Does the greater knowledge of the group's breadth of experience revealed by the exercise pique their interest in planning field trips or community exploration?

   d. How does what is excluded from the maps say as much about the mapmakers as what is included?

   e. What special experiences have the participants had with or in the places identified on the map?

   f. What does this exercise say about your community?

This exercise can lead into a discussion of many diversity-related issues. Much will depend on the nature of the city and the special perspectives of the participants. Memorable discussions have evolved from these questions:

o Why and how do ethnic enclaves develop? Under what circumstances can outsiders enter?

o Why do some people know the location of every major shopping mall in a 20-mile radius?

o Who has sports stadiums on their maps (and who doesn't)?

o Are any gay establishments or other gay landmarks noted?

o Why would someone want to spend an afternoon in a Japanese garden?

o What is your comfort level on entering a community different from your own?

Further Reading/References

Gardner, H. *Frames of the Mind: Theories of Multiple Intelligences.* New York: Basic Books, 1983.

Johnson D., and R. Johnson. *Circles of Learning: Cooperative Learning in the Classroom.* Washington, DC: ASCD, 1984.

Cooperative Map

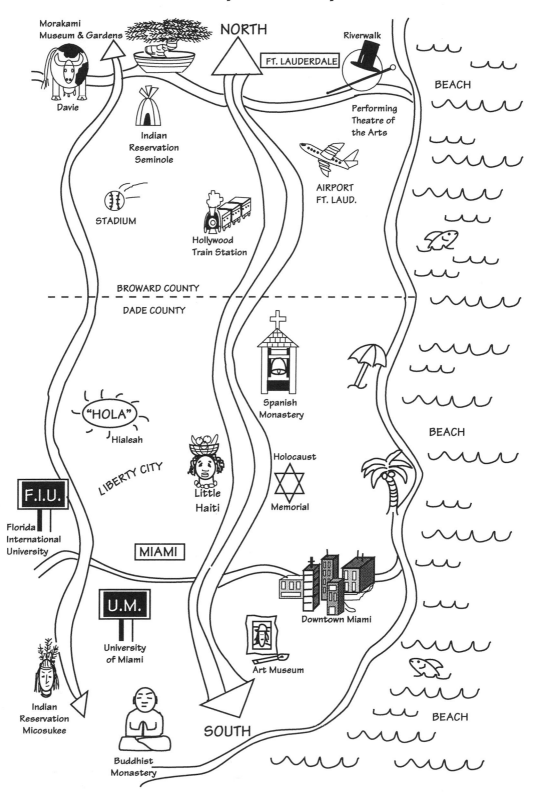

NORTH

Morakami Museum & Gardens

Davie

FT. LAUDERDALE

Riverwalk

BEACH

Indian Reservation Seminole

Performing Theatre of the Arts

STADIUM

AIRPORT FT. LAUD.

Hollywood Train Station

BROWARD COUNTY

DADE COUNTY

Spanish Monastery

"HOLA"

Hialeah

LIBERTY CITY

Little Haiti

Holocaust Memorial

F.I.U.

Florida International University

BEACH

MIAMI

U.M.

University of Miami

Downtown Miami

Art Museum

Indian Reservation Micosukee

SOUTH

BEACH

Buddhist Monastery

19

Realistic Expectations: The American Overseas Experience

Judith M. Blohm and Michael C. Mercil

Objective

False expectations are a major cause of shortened or unhappy overseas experiences. This exercise is designed to assist persons preparing to go abroad in gathering information that will bring their expectations more closely in line with reality.

Participants

Any number of persons preparing to go abroad.

Staff

Leader plus 4-6 panelists.

Materials

3 x 5 cards, pens or pencils, long table, chairs.

Setting

Panel presentation.

Time

1 hour: Introduction and question writing (10 minutes), panel presentation (30 minutes), answering selected questions (20 minutes). This exercise is especially designed for programs that have a minimum amount of time, but recognize the necessity of at least beginning the process of orienting the participants toward realistic expectations.

Procedure

1. The leader selects panel to include people who have had substantive overseas experiences (similar to those anticipated by the participants) and who are articulate and insightful in discussing them.

2. The leader poses five or so prepared questions to the panelists in advance of the session. The questions should be crafted not to elicit advice but to stimulate the panel to describe their own experiences in a way that will produce the maximum amount of useful information. Panelists are asked to be succinct, descriptive, and honest and contribute to the development among the participants of the desired realistic expectations.

   Give each question to two or more panelists, but not necessarily to all of them. It is important to get varied perspectives on each of the issues but not to get bogged down in any one and find time has run out before achieving your goals.

   Here are examples of the kinds of questions which are fruitful in this kind of exercise. These are geared to students going abroad, but a list can easily be developed for different age groups and professionals.
   a. How did your lifestyle change from what it was at home?
   b. What were your most difficult adjustments?
   c. Did you have any special communication problems and how did you deal with them?
   d. What differences, if any, did you find in the social life you encountered? How did you meet your social needs?
   e. What are the most important things you learned from the overseas experience?
   f. How has the experience continued to affect you?
3. The leader introduces the session by saying something like "This is an opportunity to hear about the experiences of some people who have been abroad on programs similar to those you are contemplating. The session will begin with a panel discussion of specific topics, then answer other questions proposed by the participants." The leader then briefly introduces the panelists.

   Distribute 3 x 5 cards and pens or pencils as required. Ask the participants to use the card at any time during the panel to write a question or identify an issue related to an aspect of their future overseas experience about which they feel most uncertain or worried.

   Ask any other persons in the audience with overseas experience to identify themselves. Suggest that these people are good resources, too. During the break, get their names and addresses so they can be contacted individually by interested participants.
4. When the panel ends, retrieve the audience questions and sort rapidly through them, grouping those that are common to more than one participant and discarding those already answered. Time may permit only a few questions, so the most interesting or the broadest ones should be chosen first.

Important: While this exercise is designed for programs with limited time available, if you have more time, by all means stretch it out. It is a rich format and if the panelists have been carefully selected, they will have much, much more of importance to say than can possibly be encompassed in an hour.

If you are on a short time leash, schedule this just before a meal or a break where participants may informally follow up with the panelists. Carefully select panelists to reflect the possible variations on the type of overseas experiences of the audience (i.e., long and short programs, rural and urban living, academic or professional programs, etc.) as well as those who express themselves effectively. In selecting and briefing the panelists, discuss format and questions with them in advance and make it clear that they are not expected to offer advice but rather to talk about their own experiences.

5. At the close of the session thank the panelists.

Further Reading/References

Educational and Training Services. *American Overseas Handbook.* Washington, DC: Youth for Understanding, 1989.

————. *Roots and Wings: American Student Orientation Workbook.* Washington, DC: Youth for Understanding, 1990.

Kalb, Rosalind, and Penelope Welch. *Moving Your Family Overseas.* Yarmouth, ME: Intercultural Press, 1992.

Kohls, L. Robert. *Survival Kit for Overseas Living.* 3d ed. Yarmouth, ME: Intercultural Press, 1996.

This activity was prepared by Judith M. Blohm and Michael C. Mercil. It appears in Judith M. Blohm and Michael C. Mercil, *Planning and Conducting Pre-Departure Orientations.* Washington, DC: Youth for Understanding, (1985): 71–72.

Section IV: Working Together (activities 20-24)

Introduction

In physics there is a principle that states that contacts between surfaces have properties quite independent of the materials involved. "They are properties that turn out to depend on the fractal quality of the bumps upon bumps...surfaces in contact do not touch everywhere," observes James Gleick in *Chaos* (NY: Penguin Books, 1987, 106).

The analogy to human contact—especially intercultural contact—is apparent. How do we enable people from distinct cultural backgrounds to touch in enough places to ensure a functioning work group?

Carol Wolf presents a simple two-step exercise to get people to clarify their personal and institutional work values.

In an approach to encouraging participants to value workplace diversity, Donna L. Goldstein divides participants into small groups, then provides one or more hypothetical candidates for inclusion (e.g., wheelchair-bound, grew up in inner city). The groups discuss unique ways these candidates might enhance the group's effectiveness. Many trainers will be inspired to tailor the list of candidates to better fit their own training circumstances.

Paula Chu provides a tool—questionnaires designed for identifying your individual and organizational cultures. The individual's responses are charted in a "compass" in which four dimensions of culture are noted: activity (doing, being, becoming); time (past, present, future); human relationships (individual, mutual, ranked); and environment/nature (yielding, harmonious, controlling).

In "Racism 101," Ellen Summerfield launches a project to uncover campus racism. She begins by showing a documentary film on racism in U.S. colleges, then divides the participants into four groups, each to look for signs of racism in different areas (i.e., social interaction in the cafeteria, admission practices, experiences of minority students, document review). This activity can be an eye-opener for mainstream students who think racism is a thing of the past.

Mary D. Imanishi shares a six-hour experiential seminar she developed for Japanese and American employees in joint-venture subsidiaries of U.S. Steel and

Kobe Steel. She began by doing an extensive needs assessment, then tested the materials in both Japan and the United States. The starting point for each one-hour session is a critical incident involving a misunderstanding between an American and a Japanese employee. Imanishi suggests four or five specific questions to be asked the participants after each incident by a facilitator knowledgeable in both cultures. Actual situations are depicted, situations in which intercultural miscommunication frequently occurs between Japanese and Americans.

20

Work Values Exercise

Carol Wolf

Objectives

- o To get people to think and talk about their own values and life histories as they relate to work, including the cultural patterns embodied therein.
- o To explore the ways in which the group or organization reflects or stimulates conflict with the values of individual members or subgroups.
- o To engage in values clarification (individual and group).

Setting

Sufficient space for large- and small-group discussions.

Participants

Individual, small groups (3-5), or large group.

Time

1 hour.

Materials

Flip chart, markers. Participants need pen and paper. Handouts 1 and 2.

Rationale

Diverse groups of people often have very different ideas about the meaning and purpose of work. Some of these differences are culturally based, others may stem from different life experiences. Quite often, these differences are unspoken, or even outside of awareness—yet they are often the root of assumptions, judgments, and conflicts in the workplace. Understanding personal and organizational value systems is a critical component in the development of diversity awareness and the bringing about of organizational change. Highlighting core organizational values, or uncovering what may be unspoken or hidden values, can help groups and individuals to better understand what enables (or disables) teamwork and effective organizational alignment. The "Work Values Exercise" helps participants take the first steps in building a foundation based on the valuing of diverse perspectives and skills. (Note: The group must be at a point in their development where open dialogue about differences is acceptable.)

Procedure

1. Have participants break into small groups (3-4 members each). Ask them to respond to and discuss their answers to each of the questions listed in Handout 1. (Approximately 20 minutes. Facilitator should make sure they don't get stuck on the first subject.) In the meantime, put the definition of "value" on a flip chart and post the list of work values.

2. Distribute Handout 2. Based on their previous discussions, ask participants to pick their three most important values from Handout 2 and, continuing in their groups, do all or some of the following:

   a. Talk about the values they chose, why they picked them, and what they mean for them.

   b. Discuss how they believe their values differ from the values of their group (organization) as a whole.

   c. Talk about what needs to change in order for them to feel more comfortable with/committed to the group.

Debriefing

1. Facilitator should observe carefully the style of decision making, assumption of group roles, communication patterns—i.e., the group process in the small groups—to determine the dynamic of each. Use this information to facilitate discussion of the ways that culture and class have an impact on the work attitudes and values the participants have been discussing. In heterogeneous groups, patterns will generally emerge along gender, racial/ethnic, and social class patterns in which the participants were raised.

2. Expand discussion by asking people how these experiences have affected their career paths, and whether these values are part of their current jobs.

Sample Questions

a. Are your values reflected in the group's values? Please explain.

b. How are your values reflected in the group? What values are they? What purpose do they serve?

c. Do you notice similarities/differences based on culture? Age? Gender?

d. Ideally, what should the group's values be? How can you move from the real toward the ideal?

Outcomes

Information gleaned from this exercise can be used as lead-in to a variety of areas, including improving reward and motivation policies, evaluating employee performance, improving team building, diagnosing work conflicts, or clarifying group identity.

Handout 1

Questions

1. When was the first time in your life that you worked? Describe what you did. How did you know it was work?

2. What was positive about this experience? What was negative?

3. What did you learn from this and subsequent experiences about yourself and work? (For example, why you work, what you need in order to work well.)

4. What messages or lessons did you get from your family about work? Who taught you? How?

Examples

"I learned that I can't stand tedious jobs" (work value: variety).
"I learned that the people I work with are important" (work value: relationships).

<u>Handout 2</u>

Definition of "Value"

A principle or quality intrinsically valuable or desirable (Webster's Ninth New Collegiate Dictionary).

Work Values

Respect

Communication

Clear purpose

Relationships—working with others

Individual achievement

Challenging work

Contribution to goals/sense of accomplishment

Recognition

Rewards

Security

Chance to develop/improve

Efficiency

Good pay/benefits

Variety of work

Control over work

Environment/surroundings

Others:

21

What Do They Bring?

Donna L. Goldstein

Objectives

1. To help participants in a work group develop greater empathy.
2. To better appreciate the value that diverse individuals bring to classrooms and organizations.

Participants

6-100+.

Materials

Work sheets, flip chart, markers, Handout: The Value of Diversity for Option B participants.

Rationale

This is an introductory exercise which would be most beneficial for people who have had little exposure to diversity training or intercultural theory. Managers are often asked to "value diversity" while many may have led insular lives and may be accustomed to living and working in homogeneous groups and settings. This may no longer be possible: The changing demographics of the workplace and our cities are impossible to ignore.

This exercise challenges groups and individuals to uncover benefits and strengths in people whose backgrounds may be different from their own. It asks them to move beyond stereotypes like "redneck" or "spoiled rich kid." It encourages them to empathize with the difficulties of learning a new language, losing one's job, or being mobility-impaired and to respect the skills developed in the process. Each person in an organization has a unique contribution to make to the whole. This activity, though begun with hypothetical employees, can help managers recognize, value, and better utilize the skills of their staff.

Procedure

There are several ways to lead this activity, depending on the number of participants and time constraints. If you have 30 or more participants, follow Option A; if you have fewer than 30, follow Option B.

Option A—(30 or more participants)

1. Divide large group into 15 smaller groups of 3-4 participants. Try to put participants who might benefit from working together after the session is over in the same group. One way to do this is to ask the participants to form their own groups of those they do not know well but with whom they might like to work.
2. Groups are numbered off 1-15.
3. The handout is distributed, and groups are assigned the (hypothetical) individual on the work sheet with his or her corresponding number; i.e., Group 1 has "A person who was one of 10 children."
4. The group's task is to think of as many valuable assets as possible that the person might bring to his or her (select the gender) classroom or organization. Example: "This person might be more able to share resources, or be more sensitive to the needs of others." One group member should note the responses.
5. When the groups have completed the task, they report one at a time to the large group summing up the group's responses, which the facilitator lists on a flip chart.
6. Discussion questions can be drawn from key points in the process. A few to consider:
   a. How did you initially feel about the person you were assigned? Did you feel any different when you were finished?
   b. How much do you know about the people in your classroom/organization?
   c. What other kinds of people should be included in this exercise?
   d. What would happen if diversity were suddenly eliminated in your organization?
   e. What are the implications that you have discovered for valuing diversity?

Option B—(29 or fewer participants)

1. Divide the large group into smaller groups of 3 participants (heterogeneous, if possible).
2. Each group gets the handout listing 15 individuals. Their task is to brainstorm and list on the sheet at least three ways that each individual with his or her particular background or characteristics could contribute to the classroom or organization (about 15-20 minutes).
3. When groups have completed the task, the facilitator brings up the individuals, one by one, and solicits input from the various groups as to their responses. The responses are written on a prepared flip chart.

4. When the potential contributions of each of the ten individuals have been discussed, the exercise can be processed, using material generated in the discussion and/or some of the following.

   a. Were there some individuals you had more difficulty with than others? Why?

   b. What were some of the perspectives presented by other groups that your group did not recognize?

   c. Who else would you have wanted to include?

   d. Will this activity motivate you to any new action? Attitude?

   e. What are the implications for valuing diversity in your organization?

   f. How could you adapt this activity to meet other learning styles?

Trainer Notes

I first got the idea for this exercise from Dr. Robert Hayles during a session he gave at SIETAR (International Society for Intercultural Education, Training and Research) in 1991. I have since modified and adapted it in several ways to achieve a variety of goals with groups of educators and executives. It has been helpful as a way to get people thinking and talking about diversity issues in a nonthreatening manner.

The example of a person from a large family, for instance, can easily lead into discussions about personal space, privacy, sharing, cooperation, and other culturally determined values. You can also ask, "Have you ever known or worked with someone who was once homeless?" Each individual's characteristics could potentially bring out many skills which might be untapped or unappreciated by the organization.

This exercise can also be helpful in causing people to examine stereotypes and assumptions. Do we assume that people from large families are poor or uneducated? Have we considered the intercultural skills a former flight attendant might possess? (My view of nuns was changed forever by one who became a dancer/choreographer).

A challenge in processing this exercise is to keep focused on the positive–the skills and benefits. Certainly there are difficulties which need to be addressed–some of these individuals may be protected by the Americans with Disabilities Act (ADA), and appropriate accommodations must be made. You will see lots of "light bulbs" going off if you keep the tone upbeat and contribute occasional suggestions yourself regarding the many benefits of diversity.

Further Reading

Hayles, Robert. *Multicultural Workforce: Issues and Opportunities.* Paper presented at the 14th annual conference of the Arizona Affirmative Action Association, Phoenix, AZ, May 1989.

Simon, G., C. Vazquez, and P. Harris. *Transcultural Leadership: Empowering the Diverse Workforce.* Houston: Gulf, 1993.

Thiederman, S. *Bridging Barriers for Corporate Success: How to Manage the Multicultural Workforce.* New York: Lexington Books, 1991.

Handout: The Value of Diversity

What would each of these people bring to an organization?
1. One of ten children
2. Grew up in inner city
3. Wheelchair-bound
4. Born outside United States; nonnative speaker
5. Only child
6. Once was homeless
7. Hearing-impaired
8. Grew up on farm, far from nearest town
9. Independently wealthy
10. Single mother of four
11. Vietnam veteran
12. Haitian or Salvadorian refugee
13. Former flight attendant
14. Former priest or nun
15. Speaks two or more languages

22

The Culture Compass
Paula Chu

Objectives

The purpose of the Culture Compass is:

o to help you understand four dimensions for measuring worldviews
o to make you aware of unconscious assumptions that you and your coworkers make which may affect your interactions
o to help you assess the culture of your organization and some of the ways that culture may affect its employees
o to enable you to use this awareness toward maximizing communication and organizational effectiveness

Participants

Any number; can be done in a group or individually.

Materials

Pencil, handouts, overhead projector (optional).

Time

60-90 minutes, including discussion.

Theoretical Background

The Culture Compass relies on a conceptual framework for defining culture on two levels. Both levels of the compass affect your work every day and in every interpersonal context. First, on a personal level:

> Culture or world view is defined as the manner in which a person perceives his or her relationship to nature, institutions, other people, and things (Sue, 1981).

Then, on an organizational level:

> [Culture is] a pattern of basic assumptions—invented, discovered, or developed by a given group as it learns to cope with its problems of external adaptation and internal integration—that has worked well enough to be considered valid and, therefore, to be taught to new members as the correct way to perceive, think, and feel in relation to those problems (Schein 1985).

The Culture Compass allows you to explore four dimensions of culture or worldview. These are:

a. orientation toward activity

b. orientation toward time

c. orientation toward human relationships

d. orientation toward the environment/nature

Part 1 of the Culture Compass focuses on identifying your individual culture. The descriptions of cultural assumptions which follow will sketch aspects of the worldview which you most consciously endorse.

Part 2 of the Culture Compass focuses on identifying the organizational culture that you feel operates in a particular work setting. In this context, the descriptions which follow will sketch assumptions that you feel are *generally considered correct by people who most strongly influence and define your organizational culture*. Implications include:

o what behaviors are rewarded and in what way

o who "fits" in the organization

o how employees are expected to interact

o the pace of the workday

o relationship to organization's own history, its present reality, and its future goals

o relationship to the influences and constraints of its own environment

o degree of appreciation for differing worldviews, cooperation, and the value of collective diversity

It may be helpful to you as facilitator to know that research has determined that there exists a fifth dimension which shapes our worldviews, and that has to do with how we view *human nature*. Is humankind good, evil, or a combination of the two? For the sake of the simplicity of the Culture Compass and its utility as a discussion tool, this dimension is not included. However, you may wish to raise it in discussion and have participants consider ways in which their organization(s) may differ from themselves as individuals in terms of assumptions about human nature. Are people seen as inherently lazy or industrious? Selfish or generous? Trustworthy or not trustworthy? How do these affect hiring, promotion? What kinds of behavior are rewarded based on these assumptions? Who are the "organizational heroes and villains" (Schein 1985)?

Trainer Tips

The Culture Compass was designed as a tool to enhance and help structure the discussion of cultural differences in the workplace. Each participant is asked to rate a series of statements related to his or her own worldview: Which of these statements is *most like me, next most like me, least like me?* Participants are then asked to fill out the Organizational Culture Compass, rating statements as they reflect the particular organization culture in which they operate: Which of these statements is *most dominant in the organization, next most dominant, least dominant?*

As facilitator, you need to give participants an overview of the dimensions of worldview that the Culture Compass is designed to reflect. Be sure to list for the group the objectives given above. It is often helpful to have overheads prepared which provide the definitions of "culture" or "worldview" on both individual and organizational levels.

Provide sufficient time to fill out the compasses (15-25 minutes), and then show them how to score their responses and record them in graphic form. Encourage those who have finished early to read the descriptions of the worldview dimensions and to make note of some of the ways in which descriptions ring true for them as well as ways in which they do not ring true.

Discussion afterward is often most useful in small groups, which later report back to the larger group. Be sure to include everyone in the conversation—each person's perceptions of cultural differences and norms in the organization are valid and should be respected as such. You may wish to establish some ground rules before discussion begins. Helpful ones may include:

- Speak from your own experience
- No verbal attacks on individuals
- Maintain confidentiality outside the workshop
- Respect different perspectives
- Be honest

Participants may have ground rules of their own to propose. You may in fact have an interesting discussion about the issue of ground rules themselves. Who sets them in the organization and what aspect of the organizational worldview do they reflect?

Procedure

1. Have participants fill out the questionnaires in Handout 1: Personal Perspective and Handout 2: Organizational Norms. Allow enough time, probably 15-25 minutes.
2. Distribute Handout 3: Profile of Cultural Perspectives. Allow 5-10 minutes for participants to read.
3. Lead discussion of the results of the questionnaires.

The questions below are most useful in a small-group setting for initiating discussions. Large groups may wish to break down into smaller groups and then come together for a summary discussion. You may wish to ask only one or two questions in a given session, as each may generate considerable discussion.

a. How did you describe your own culture? The organizational culture? What differences did you perceive between organizational worldviews and your own?

b. Discuss an encounter or relationship in which someone's cultural perspective appears to be different from your own or a situation where there appears to be a conflict between the perceived organizational culture and your own. Share your ideas on the cultural dynamic that may be operating.

c. What kinds of expectations of self and others do you see in each dimension? Give examples of interpersonal and work expectations.

d. What kinds of things could holders of each worldview do to show respect and appreciation for differing worldviews?

e. What kinds of things could be done to support the work of someone who holds each of the worldviews? Note: Large groups may wish to assign teams of a few individuals to generate ideas for each of the four orientation compass dimensions (i.e., activity, time, human relationships, relationship to environment/nature).

f. What kinds of conflicts have you seen at work between/among people who hold specific worldviews? Describe both process and result of the conflict you have in mind.

g. Within many organizations, different cultural worldviews operate in different departments. In what ways do you see this dynamic within your organization?

h. Talk about the process of your small-group discussion itself. To what extent and in what manner are different cultural worldviews operating? What other issues are influencing the discussion (e.g., race, class, ethnicity, nationality, gender)?

i. Select a cross-cultural situation described by one of your group members and generate ideas about how the situation could be affected in a positive way based on cultural awareness.

j. Within a cultural framework, what is your role in the total organizational culture? In what ways do your behavior and awareness of cultural assumptions have an impact on your work relationships? In what specific ways would you like to diversify your responses to situations involving worldview differences?

4. Probe participant satisfaction. The facilitator debriefs the participants by asking:
   a. To what extent do you think the cultural profile provided by your individual compass is accurate? Your institution's profile?
   b. What value is there for you in exploring this issue and its dynamics?

Further Reading/References

Ibrahim F. A., and H. Kahn. "Scale to Assess World Views across Cultures." Storrs, CT: University of Connecticut, unpublished, 1984.

———. *Assessment of World Views. Psychological Reports, 60,* 1987: 163–76.

Kluckhohn, F., and F. Strodtbeck. *Variations in Value Orientations*. New York: Harper and Row, 1961. For information on the theoretical rationale for Culture Compass dimensions.

Schein, E. H. *Organizational Culture and Leadership: A Dynamic View*. San Francisco: Jossey-Bass, 1985.

Sue, D. W. *Counseling the Culturally Different: Theory and Practice*. New York: John Wiley, 1981.

Handout 1: Personal Perspective

Part 1. Rank the following according to similarity to your own perspective.

    3 - most like me

    2 - next most like me

    1 - least like me

1. _____ a. My decisions are primarily guided by what I have learned.
    _____ b. I "go with the flow" and adapt my decisions to quickly changing circumstances.
    _____ c. When I make a decision, I focus on the result I am looking for.

2. _____ a. I tend to take each day as it comes.
    _____ b. I tend to keep lists of tasks that I need to accomplish each day.
    _____ c. In time, things do tend to work themselves out.

3. _____ a. It is hard for me to stop worrying about upcoming events or deadlines.
    _____ b. Life has its own wisdom. Worrying is a waste of my energy.
    _____ c. Let's focus on all that today brings, and take care of the rest one day at a time.

4. _____ a. We are meant to attend to nature's needs as much as to our own.
    _____ b. Humanity's progress and survival depend on our control of natural resources.
    _____ c. Nature's own power will determine our progress and survival; humanity's power can neither match it nor truly control it.

5. _____ a. In truth, we are much better off now that we can make more effective use of our natural resources.
    _____ b. For all our great plans and projects, nature could put humankind in its place in an instant.
    _____ c. "Effective use of natural resources" is the same as saying "exploitation of the natural world."

6. _____ a. No matter where you live, in the country or the city, there are a variety of forces operating which control your destiny.
    _____ b. In my life, I strive to live simply, which is closer to the natural world.
    _____ c. Modern conveniences actually help us appreciate the natural world.

7. _____ a. Developing my potential and my sense of self is the most important thing I can do with my life.

_____ b. Being alive and healthy is the most important thing to me; my accomplishments are secondary.

_____ c. It would be a waste if I did not achieve something important in my life.

8. _____ a. I prefer to relax and enjoy life as it comes.

_____ b. Peace of mind is possible regardless of external circumstances.

_____ c. I feel useless if I'm not doing something constructive with my time.

9. _____ a. Taking action is more important than commitment to a belief.

_____ b. We exist only in relation to other people.

_____ c. It is essential to be a good person; being a successful person is not the point.

10. _____ a. You've got to be guided by what you think is right, even if you can't please everyone.

_____ b. It works best to have a good leader make the decisions; everyone should cooperate accordingly.

_____ c. Decisions affecting a group are more effective if everyone participates in the decision making.

11. _____ a. It is the individual I respect—not his or her position.

_____ b. Leaders of a group deserve respect because of their position.

_____ c. First and foremost comes unity; people who think of themselves first live at the expense of others.

12. _____ a. The head of a group has to take responsibility for its success or failure.

_____ b. If someone in my group is having a problem, I am partly responsible for resolving it.

_____ c. I am accountable for my own success or failure.

Now score your Individual Culture Compass.

Place the number recorded beside each statement in the appropriate space below and add at the right.

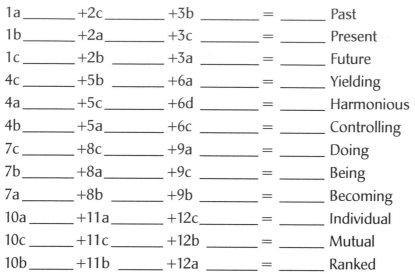

1a _____ +2c _____ +3b _____ = _____ Past

1b _____ +2a _____ +3c _____ = _____ Present

1c _____ +2b _____ +3a _____ = _____ Future

4c _____ +5b _____ +6a _____ = _____ Yielding

4a _____ +5c _____ +6d _____ = _____ Harmonious

4b _____ +5a _____ +6c _____ = _____ Controlling

7c _____ +8c _____ +9a _____ = _____ Doing

7b _____ +8a _____ +9c _____ = _____ Being

7a _____ +8b _____ +9b _____ = _____ Becoming

10a _____ +11a _____ +12c _____ = _____ Individual

10c _____ +11c _____ +12b _____ = _____ Mutual

10b _____ +11b _____ +12a _____ = _____ Ranked

Mark the number corresponding to your score for each subdimension on the Individual Culture Compass. You may wish to shade in each section to the appropriate level. The highest number for each dimension indicates your preferred approach.

Individual Culture Compass

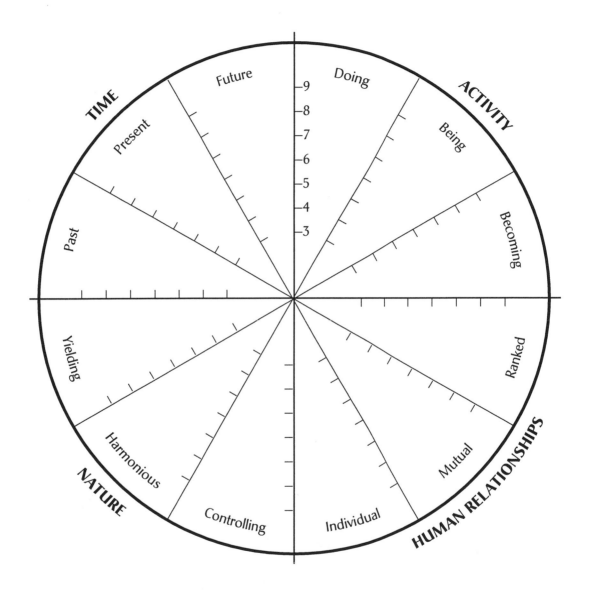

Handout 2: Organizational Norms

Part 2. Rank the following norms or perspectives according to their dominance at your organization or institution.

   3 - most dominant

   2 - next most dominant

   1 - least dominant

1. _____ a.   Priorities and strategies are based on tradition and what experience has shown to work.

   _____ b.   People tend to "go with the flow."

   _____ c.   Priorities and strategies are based on careful consideration of future goals.

2. _____ a.   The organization as a whole does not emphasize future goals; how we are doing now is more important.

   _____ b.   The organization has clear short- and long-term goals which guide the daily work.

   _____ c.   There is a strong sense of the legacy of the organization and its history.

3. _____ a.   In general, there is considerable anxiety about upcoming events or deadlines.

   _____ b.   There is a great deal of pride in the organization's past accomplishments and reputation.

   _____ c.   People in the organization enjoy its current state and tend not to worry too much about its future.

4. _____ a.   The organization's primary purpose is to contribute to society.

   _____ b.   The organization's progress and survival depend on its taking advantage of economic, political, and other opportunities and resources.

   _____ c.   The organization is relatively powerless in the larger scheme of things.

5. _____ a.   Effective management and use of resources enable the organization to influence and control its destiny.

   _____ b.   The organization has little control given the many constraints under which it must operate.

   _____ c.   The organization has a mutually beneficial relationship with its political, economic, and social environments.

6. _____ a. The organization is seen as a small cog in a very complex machine.

_____ b. The organization exists to cooperate with and further the goals of its environment.

_____ c. In our organization, it is believed that we can achieve our goals through hard work, perseverance, and seizing opportunities as they arise.

7. _____ a. The organization emphasizes employee development.

_____ b. Lots of people who work here just plain enjoy it.

_____ c. Getting the job done is the top priority.

8. _____ a. If we run into a difficulty or problem, it is assumed that things will work themselves out.

_____ b. Problems which arise here are seen as a natural part of the growth and development of any organization; everyone has his or her role in resolving them.

_____ c. If a difficulty arises, it must be resolved immediately; ignoring it is seen as counterproductive.

9. _____ a. What the organization stands for is considered less important than getting one's work done well.

_____ b. People work here because the work being done is important.

_____ c. Everyone is encouraged to be him- or herself; that is our best contribution to the work we do.

10. _____ a. Each of us makes decisions based on what seems right.

_____ b. Those in positions of authority make the decisions; everyone else follows these directives.

_____ c. Decision making is, for the most part, a collective process.

11. _____ a. Everyone here is considered worthy of equal respect.

_____ b. Those at the top of the hierarchy are worthy of respect because of their positions.

_____ c. In a working environment such as ours, people who try to gain for themselves alone do so at the expense of others.

12. _____ a. The head of the department guides the rest of the unit and takes responsibility for its successes and failures.

_____ b. If someone has a success or failure, the responsibility is shared by others in the department.

_____ c. Each of us is held accountable for our own successes and failures.

Now score your Organizational Culture Compass.

Place the number recorded beside each statement in the appropriate space below and add at the right.

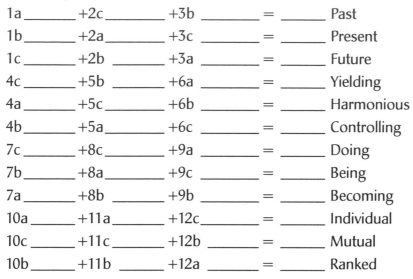

1a _____ +2c _____ +3b _____ = _____ Past

1b _____ +2a _____ +3c _____ = _____ Present

1c _____ +2b _____ +3a _____ = _____ Future

4c _____ +5b _____ +6a _____ = _____ Yielding

4a _____ +5c _____ +6b _____ = _____ Harmonious

4b _____ +5a _____ +6c _____ = _____ Controlling

7c _____ +8c _____ +9a _____ = _____ Doing

7b _____ +8a _____ +9c _____ = _____ Being

7a _____ +8b _____ +9b _____ = _____ Becoming

10a _____ +11a _____ +12c _____ = _____ Individual

10c _____ +11c _____ +12b _____ = _____ Mutual

10b _____ +11b _____ +12a _____ = _____ Ranked

Mark the number corresponding to your score for each subdimension on the Organizational Culture Compass. You may wish to shade in each section to the appropriate level. The highest number for each dimension indicates your perception of the dominant approach at your institution.

Organizational Culture Compass

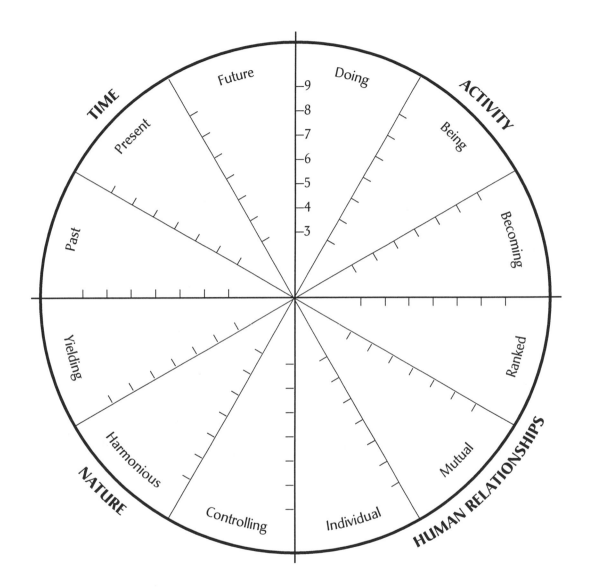

Handout 3: Profile of Cultural Perspectives

Part 3. Check your individual and organizational culture compasses against the following profile of cultural perspectives.

A. Orientation toward Activity

- Doing
- Being
- Becoming

Doing:

Assumption: Taking action is the most important activity.
Finds meaning in: Accomplishments, achievements.
Meaning of work: A "doer" *is* what he/she *does*. Work is pursued for a living (Work=Living). Relationships are secondary to the task. Work and play are separate activities, but "doers" often work hard *and* play hard.

Being

Assumption: Self-expression is the most important activity.
Finds meaning in: Spontaneous expression, being oneself, affiliation.
Meaning of work: Work is not directly attached to the ego, nor is it strictly considered a separate activity from leisure. Social and work relationships may be closely intertwined. Relationship development at work is time well spent; it builds morale and group identity/feeling.

Becoming

Assumption: Self-development is the most important activity.
Finds meaning in: Process, purpose and intention of activity.
Meaning of work: There is a deep investment in the *type of work* and its process; both aspects add to one's personal development.

B. Orientation toward Time

- Past
- Present
- Future

Past

Assumption: Today flows out of the legacy of the past.
Finds meaning in: Serenity, surrender, history as context and teacher.
Meaning of work: Work is a place to establish and nurture relationships and traditions. There is an awareness of, connection to, and obligation toward the legacy of such relationships and traditions.

Present

Assumption: Today is the only reality.
Finds meaning in: *Carpe diem* ("seize the day").
Meaning of work: Work, like life, is to be enjoyed. Present-oriented individuals often bring to work an energy and vitality not as frequently embodied by the other orientations.

Future

Assumption: Today is a step toward tomorrow's goals.
Finds meaning in: Establishing and working toward goals, work ethic.
Meaning of work: Finds his/her identity through achievements in the workplace. Keeps one eye on deadlines and goals and evaluates the present in relation to its utility in moving toward the future. Is rarely satisfied with achievements, focusing on the next. Endorses ethic of "no pain, no gain."

C. Orientation toward Human Relationships

- Individual
- Ranked
- Mutual

Individual

Assumption: Each person is responsible for what happens in his or her life, and must watch out for his or her own rights and welfare.
Finds meaning in: Personal accountability, competitive ethic.
Meaning of work: Work is a place to be recognized for one's own achievements. Upward mobility and other forms of recognition are expected from these individuals; group goals, rewards, and achievements are not as satisfying.

Ranked

Assumption: Each of us has his or her own place, and respect is due according to one's position.
Finds meaning in: Tradition, hierarchy, family, protocol.
Meaning of work: Work is a place to enhance or strengthen, but not necessarily advance, one's social position. Protocol is seen as maintaining the weave of the social fabric. There is a higher value placed on being respectful than on being frank.

Mutual

Assumption: My purpose is to make a contribution to a larger whole.
Finds meaning in: Interdependence, group goals, affiliation.
Meaning of work: Work is a place to make a contribution to a group effort. The mutual individual needs to have a sense of belonging to projects and to see the connection to a larger goal or effort. Public praise and competition among or comparison to others may cause embarrassment.

D. Orientation toward the environment/nature

○ Controlling
○ Yielding
○ Harmonious

Controlling

Assumption: Human welfare is primary; nature serves to meet our needs.
Finds meaning in: Taking charge of challenges, mind over matter, effective use of resources.
Meaning of work: Work is a place to manage and control tasks, resources, employees. Problems are to be solved, knots in the system to be untied, hurdles to be jumped or dismantled.

Yielding

Assumption: Nature is in charge of life on earth.
Finds meaning in: Nature rules humankind, we have little control.
Meaning of work: Work must be done. Within an organization, such individuals may feel dominated by the organization and try to adapt to their roles and assignments rather than influence them.

Harmony with Nature

Assumption: Our relationship with nature is symbiotic; care for the physical world will pay off with a balanced and peaceful existence.
Finds meaning in: Harmony, doing one's share.
Meaning of work: Work is part of a contract of balance wherein people contribute their share toward a symbiotic relationship with society, nature, and all aspects of life.

23

Racism 101

Ellen Summerfield

Objective

To make racial attitudes and racism visible to U.S. students by directing their attention to social interactions in the cafeteria, to admissions and hiring practices, to the personal experiences of "minority" students and faculty, and to selected university documents and literature (e.g., campus newspaper, university bylaws and mission statement, and recruitment materials).

Participants

Any number; divide into small groups of 3-6.

Materials

Notebook and pencil.

Setting

University or college campus; can be adapted easily to other organizational settings. Activity can be done individually or by small groups (see instructions below).

Time

60-90 minutes for orientation and film; several days for fieldwork; 10-20 minutes for each small-group report on findings; 30-50 minutes for large-group debriefing.

Rationale

Educators wishing to help students learn more about racial attitudes and racism have a powerful tool at their disposal: film. Film can provide entry into topics that seem too controversial, too uncomfortable for many educators to handle in other ways. It breaks through barriers, giving students permission to do the same; as they think and talk about a film, they are, of course, really talking about themselves—but in a form that is indirect and, thus, relatively safe. A film such as *Racism*

101, which addresses black-white relations in forthright terms, helps students over-come their own inhibitions or reluctance to talk about racial issues. They begin to gain confidence in their ability to express themselves on sensitive matters; they can test their views and begin to learn how others think and react.

Trainer Tips

This exercise may not be suitable for all groups and classes. Facilitators should assess maturity level and preparedness of the class members before attempting it. The *sequencing* of multicultural materials is of paramount importance, and it is almost always advisable to begin conservatively and then move to more contro-versial areas. Once a sense of trust develops, facilitators can venture into more challenging territory.

Since the term "minority" has become problematic, facilitators may wish to sub-stitute other terminology. At the very least, students should be made aware that the term itself is controversial.

While this exercise is primarily intended for "majority" students, on whom it will likely have the greatest impact, members of minority groups can participate fully and generally learn a great deal as well—about their own ethnic, racial, or national group; about another minority group; or about the dominant culture. Minority-group members can also play an important role as cultural informants, helping others to see, understand, and take seriously the situation of those who experience discrimination. International students can add an interesting and important dimen-sion to the investigations as well as to follow-up discussions.

While analyses and discussions will usually focus on negative attitudes and discriminatory behavior, facilitators can help students discover and discuss posi-tive signs, attitudes, and behaviors as well. As we work toward racial justice and equality, looking at possible solutions is undoubtedly as important as examining the problems themselves.

Before the exercise is concluded, the students individually can be invited to formulate at least one concrete step they might take toward combating racism in their own lives.

Procedure

1. Facilitator begins by showing a film on racism in the United States. *Racism 101* (1988, 57 min., color, PBS Video) is especially recommended. After viewing the film, students are debriefed: What did they think of the events portrayed? Did they have an emotional reaction?

2. Facilitator explains that each student is going to explore possible signs of rac-ism on campus by doing one of four studies:

    a. Observe the patterns of social interaction in the cafeteria or snack bar by noting who sits with whom. To what extent do people seem to inter-act across racial, ethnic, and national boundaries? To what extent does there seem to be segregation, whether by choice or otherwise?

    b. Look for possible biases in college admissions practices. Does the per-centage of minority group members in the campus population match the percentage in the state or national populations? Interview the "gatekeepers" (i.e., the admissions officers) to get their perspective, and local minority leaders to get theirs. Also, look at financial aid policies for evidence of racial preference (e.g., minority scholarships) or discrimination. Similarly, students can investigate the extent and types of diversity present among faculty and staff.

c. Ask minority students or faculty to give their views on campus racism.

d. Analyze the image regarding diversity as reflected in documents such as the campus newspaper, the college mission statement and bylaws, the academic catalogue (look for statements, photographs of students, and course offerings), and affirmative action guidelines. Interview professors, department chairs, and administrative staff to get their views on how well the university's image and goals match the realities.

3. Each small group prepares a report of its procedures and findings. An oral synopsis of each report is presented to the large group.

4. Facilitator coordinates a large-group discussion of the students' findings. Were the results expected? Surprising? What are the problem areas? Are any positive steps being undertaken?

Other Suggested Films

Trouble Behind (1990, 56 min., color, California Newsreel).

Who Killed Vincent Chin? (1988, 82 min., color, Filmakers Library).

Blue Collar and Buddha (1989, 57 min., color, NAATA/Crosscurrent Media).

River People: Behind the Case of David Sohappy (1990, 50 min., color, Filmakers Library).

Ethnic Notions (1987, 56 min., color, California Newsreel).

Black History: Lost, Stolen, or Strayed (1968, 53 min., color/b/w, Phoenix/BFA Films and Video).

True Colors (1991, 19 min., color, Coronet/MTI Film and Video).

Just Black? Multi-Racial Identity (1991, 57 min., color, Filmakers Library).

Further Reading/References

Abrash, Barbara, and Catherine Egan, eds. *Mediating History: The MAP Guide to Independent Video by and about African American, Asian American, Latino, and Native American People.* New York: University Press, 1992.

Bogle, Donald. *Blacks in American Films and Television: An Encyclopedia.* New York: Garland Publishing, 1988.

Gee, Bill J. *Asian-American Media Reference Guide.* 2d ed. New York: Asian CineVision, 1990.

Miller, Randall M., ed. *The Kaleidoscopic Lens: How Hollywood Views Ethnic Groups.* Englewood, NJ: Jerome S. Ozer, 1980.

Weatherford, Elizabeth, and Emilia Seubert, eds. *Native Americans on Film and Video.* 2 vols. New York: Museum of the American Indian, 1981, 1987.

Zeigler, Lee. *Film and Video Resources for International Educational Exchange.* Washington, DC: NAFSA: Association of International Educators, 1992. Available from Intercultural Press.

This activity was put together by the editor from material in Ellen Summerfield's chapter "In Our Own Backyard: Cultures within the United States" in her book *Crossing Cultures through Film*, Yarmouth, ME: Intercultural Press (1993): 115–47. The book contains her culturally sensitive reviews of over seventy films that are good springboards to discussions on cross-cultural issues.

24

Sharing Work Space Japanese and Americans

Mary D. Imanishi

Goal

To increase understanding and awareness of some of the differences between Japanese and American workplace cultures.

Behavioral Objectives

1. Participants are able to identify differences in behavior which cause miscommunication.
2. Participants are able to explain the reason for the miscommunication in terms of value differences and perceptual differences regarding cultural roles and expectations from Japanese and American perspectives.
3. Participants are able to describe new behaviors or strategies which would improve communication for the foreign national and/or the host national.

Materials

Critical incidents, pens/pencils, flip chart.

Participants

Separate or combined groups of Japanese or American white- or blue-collar workers.

Use

1. As a supplement to cognitive-affective-based training where participants must apply their knowledge of cultural differences to determine the cause of miscommunication or misunderstanding.
2. As an introduction to cognitive-affective-based training in order to present a "problem" so as to increase the participants' need to resolve the miscommunication/misunderstanding through systematic analysis.

Method

Experiential training where participants are encouraged to develop "self-learning" skills. Instructor guides and stimulates students, rather than supplying clear-cut answers or "right" answers to problems. Instructor needs to have in-depth knowledge of U.S. and Japanese cultures.

Time

Allow 1-2 hours or more for each critical incident (there are six incidents), depending on the number, knowledge level, or level of cross-cultural experience of the participants. Generally, participants who have frequent contact with the contrasting culture easily expand on the concepts presented in the incident itself.

Background

The six critical incidents and exercises were developed as part of a comprehensive intercultural training seminar for Japanese and American employees in the United States and Japan. The content is based on the results of a countrywide needs assessment conducted at Kobe Steel's subsidiaries and joint-venture companies in the United States in 1990. The aim of the assessment was to determine specific communication and language problems most prevalent between the Japanese and their American counterparts and to help resolve those problems through intercultural awareness training. The assessment also included face-to-face interviews with both cultural groups. The information gathered provided the basis for the critical incidents and exercises which follow.

These materials have been used in a series of intercultural seminars designed in 1991 for over 160 managers and staff at USS/Kobe Steel in Lorain, Ohio—a 50-50 joint venture between Kobe Steel and USS. They have also been used in predeparture training for over 80 Japanese at the company headquarters in Japan.

Each activity has been rated very highly by both Japanese and American participants in terms of depicting actual situations in which intercultural miscommunication most frequently occurs. All the incidents are used to increase participants' analytical skills (to improve intercultural communication) following cognitive-based training on Japanese/American behavioral characteristics, value systems, assumptions, perceptual differences across cultures, and communication-style comparisons. It is assumed these materials will be used by experienced trainers who have a good knowledge of intercultural communication and who have worked/lived in Japan.

Procedure

1. Distribute handout that will provide the information for the session; there are six handouts, one for each session. All participants should carefully read through the incident or case study as well as the discussion questions that follow. Questions on vocabulary or content should be clarified as needed on an individual basis.

2. Have each participant go back through the exercise and underline the key issues or problems.

3. Divide the class in twos or threes and have each group work on the discussion questions. For a class of six or fewer, this can be done as a whole. If working with nonnative speakers, pair-work can be effective.

4. Following small-group discussions, solicit findings from various groups. List key problems and/or underlying values on a flip chart.

5. For questions on strategies, list suggestions from the group on a flip chart. Encourage participants to brainstorm to find effective approaches to handling the miscommunication. Solutions which appear to be the most obvious, i.e., learning about the cultures involved, are valid and should be emphasized as a continuous learning process.

6. These exercises can be followed up with role-play exercises which focus on the new behavior to be learned or by a comprehensive study of distinct cultural values and behaviors and their interpretations.

7. Information on the flip charts should be retained or posted for review in subsequent training sessions.

8. Participants should also follow up by using the new strategies in actual work situations. This could be done by introducing "action plans" which can be implemented on an individual or group level.

Handout 1: A "Better" Way of Doing Things in Japan

Mr. Jones has recently joined a Japanese company in Osaka. His job is to sell equipment to U.S. manufacturers. He is thirty years old and married. He is very happy to be in Japan and enjoys his work. However, he is having some difficulties in communicating with his Japanese coworkers.

For example, last week he did not have much work to do. Business has been slow and he has not received many new orders. Mr. Jones asked his Japanese boss if there was some work he could do, but his boss did not give him an answer. It seemed that everyone in his office was busy except him.

At lunchtime, one of Mr. Jones's coworkers asked him to go out drinking after work, but Mr. Jones said he could not go. He usually leaves the office at 5:30. He feels he does not need to stay late because he finishes his work on time and wants to spend the evenings with his family. He thinks the Japanese are slow workers because they have to stay in the office until 9:00 or 10:00 every night. He also thinks some of his coworkers don't care about their families very much.

Since Mr. Jones joined the company two months ago, he has seen many ways in which the work could be done more efficiently. He has given his suggestions to his boss and coworkers, but nothing has changed.

For example, he has suggested stopping the morning exercise because it wastes too much time. He also thinks meetings are too long. He suggests setting a time limit and preparing a written agenda before each meeting. He has brought up these suggestions many times, but no one gives him a direct answer. His boss only said it would be difficult, but Mr. Jones does not understand why. Mr. Jones thinks his idea is a rather simple solution to a very big problem. He thinks his suggestions will help workers return home at an earlier time.

The other day his boss gave him back a report which Mr. Jones had prepared one week earlier. His boss said he needed to rewrite it because there were some mistakes. Mr. Jones checked the report again and became angry because the boss had corrected his English. Mr. Jones complained to his boss about it in front of his coworkers. He also demanded that his boss give him more challenging work to do. His boss did not give him an answer, but told him to finish rewriting the report. Mr. Jones thinks his boss is unfair and does not treat him like a professional.

Discussion Questions

1. What are some examples of miscommunication between Mr. Jones and his coworkers/boss?
2. What is the cause of this miscommunication?
3. What values are represented in this case study?
4. What are some ways to reduce or minimize the miscommunication?

Handout 2: A "Better" Way of Doing Things in America

Mr. Matsumoto has recently been assigned to a joint-venture company in the United States. His job is to study existing plant conditions in the factory and make improvements based on the technological capacity of the parent company in Japan. The U.S. plant is old and has not been keeping pace with the technological advancements necessary to remain competitive.

Mr. Matsumoto is basically happy to be in the United States and he enjoys his work. However, he is having some difficulties communicating with his American coworkers.

For example, Mr. Matsumoto has observed that almost all the American workers go straight home after work. He is amazed that people leave their jobs on time, even if there is still a lot of work to do. In fact, the other day he asked one of the plant workers to help another guy fix a loose connection on the assembly line, but he refused. He said it wasn't his responsibility. Mr. Matsumoto was shocked that this young man would refuse to do a simple, routine task, especially for one of the managers. Mr. Matsumoto thinks American workers don't care about their jobs very much and certainly don't know how to show respect. He also thinks they are selfish and childish when they constantly complain about everything.

Since Mr. Matsumoto joined the company two months ago, he has seen many ways in which the work could be done more efficiently and productively. He has put forward his suggestions, but nothing has changed.

For example, he has suggested that each shift take part in formal exercise before beginning their work in order to establish group cooperation and mental alertness. He thinks it would also help if workers would wear uniforms, to foster a sense of pride and oneness in the company. Another big problem is the lack of housekeeping in the plant. He suggests that each person be responsible for sweeping debris, keeping handrails dust- and grease-free, and keeping water off the floor. It seems that no one wants to do any "extra" work that they were not specifically assigned. Mr. Matsumoto cannot understand why people refuse to do simple tasks that will help contribute to a safe work environment and a well-run company.

At lunchtime, he joined a group of workers from his section. They were in the middle of some serious discussion, so he remained silent so as not to disturb them. Then one of the group asked him for his opinion on the subject. Mr. Matsumoto was embarrassed and said he didn't know. Then one of the other guys asked him about his family and what he was going to do on the weekend. Mr. Matsumoto could hardly think about the weekend as it was only Wednesday and he was busy worrying about how to handle all the work he had to do. He told his coworker that he would probably work on the weekend. His coworker just laughed at him and hit him on the back a few times. Mr. Matsumoto thinks his behavior was rude and insulting. He wonders if any Americans take their work seriously.

Later in the day, one of the supervisors came up to him with a problem he was having on the assembly line with one of the feed reels. It seemed to be constantly jamming, so he wanted to know what he should do. Mr. Matsumoto was unaware that any malfunction was occurring. No one on the night shift had mentioned any irregularity to him, and no report was made. The supervisor seemed to think that the problem had just started, but he wasn't sure why it had happened. When the supervisor asked him what he should do, Mr. Matsumoto could not give him a definite answer. He said they would have to stop the machine for the time being and examine what had happened. The supervisor thinks Mr. Matsumoto does not handle problems in a timely manner. Finding the cause of the problem could take days—time they didn't have. On the other hand, Mr. Matsumoto cannot understand why the supervisor expects him to make decisions without any data or without conferring with the people who operate the machine. In his opinion, that kind of carelessness can only lead to disaster.

Finally, Mr. Matsumoto called an emergency meeting to discuss the problem. The supervisor, maintenance crew, and two operators attended the meeting. A great deal of discussion ensued, and two workers got into a big argument as to whose fault it was. Each person seemed to have his own idea as to the cause of the problem, but no one produced any report or other evidence which supported his judgment. Mr. Matsumoto could hardly follow what was being said. It seemed everyone was interested in the quickest, cheapest, and easiest solution, rather than a thorough, effective, and long-lasting one.

Mr. Matsumoto has become very unhappy about his work situation.

Discussion Questions

1. What are some examples of miscommunication between Mr. Matsumoto and his American coworkers?
2. What values are represented through the behaviors of the Japanese and American workers?
3. How do you feel about Mr. Matsumoto's perceptions about his American coworkers?
4. What are some ways to minimize the conflicts between Mr. Matsumoto and his coworkers?
5. What are some ways the company can improve its work environment and problem-solving procedures given the nature of the two distinct cultural groups in this joint venture?

Handout 3: Sticks and Stones

The following conversations take place after a department meeting at Big Star Steel Co., a joint venture between a Japanese and an American steel maker in the United States.

John and Andy

John: Can you believe those guys? Sato never said a word all afternoon. In fact, I saw him sleeping again halfway through the meeting.

Andy: Yeah, I guess he doesn't like our ideas. He just sits there with his arms folded looking bored. But I'm really surprised at Matsumoto and Takano. Usually I can talk to them real well during work time. I wonder why they were so quiet? It's like they don't want to participate.

John: Yeah, and when they do say something, it's always in Japanese. I know for a fact that Sato speaks English very well. You should have heard him after the golf game—he was even singing in English!

Andy: Well, I think they speak in Japanese because they don't want us to know what they're saying. Besides, you can never get a straight answer out of them. To tell you the truth, I don't trust them. I thought they came here to work as part of a team, but it sure doesn't look that way to me.

Sato and Takano (translated from Japanese)

Sato: Boy am I tired. I could hardly understand anything in that meeting. Why do Americans use so much slang?

Takano: I don't know, but too many guys talk all at once. I can't keep up with them. Besides, I don't want to argue all day the way they do. Mike and Jim really must not like each other—did you hear Mike yelling?

Sato: No, I must have fallen asleep. I just can't understand what's going on. It makes me very tired. Anyway, I can't give any opinion until I have all the necessary data; otherwise, it's a waste of time.

Takano: Well, every time I try to explain that to Mike, he gets angry. He always wants an immediate answer to everything.

Sato: Well, they just don't understand how to run a steel company properly. I thought they wanted to be part of a team, but it doesn't look that way to me.

Discussion Questions

1. What are some examples of miscommunication between the Japanese and the Americans in this case study?
2. How does each side perceive the other?
3. Are these perceptions valid?
4. Who is to "blame" for the miscommunication?
5. What can be done to improve the situation?

Handout 4: A "No Win" Situation?

The following comments were heard on separate occasions from a Japanese and an American worker in a joint-venture manufacturing plant in the United States.

American Worker

"I just can't understand it. Every time we have trouble with a machine breaking down in the plant, we always get the same answer from the Japanese—'We need time to check the data.' It's like they can't make any decision without taking four or five days to gather information and confer with the other Japanese workers. In the meantime, we get blamed for being behind production schedules. I thought the Japanese were highly experienced in this business, but they just can't make timely decisions. We need to keep those machines running or else we're going to be out of a job. It's hopeless."

Japanese Worker

"It's so difficult when Americans come to us for quick answers when a machine breaks down. Sure we can say how to fix the thing well enough to keep it running for the time being, but that is not the Japanese way. We need to analyze why it broke down in the first place to prevent such a problem from happening again. We think it is better to fix the problem properly in the beginning than to wait for it to happen again. Maybe Americans don't care about the long-term effect. Why keep fixing the same old problem over and over—which then creates some bigger problem later on—if we can modify the machine or make adjustments now to make it more efficient and dependable? There seems to be little emphasis on quality and team effort. I wish workers would care more about the future of this company."

Discussion Questions

1. What are some examples of the different ways the Americans and the Japanese solve problems?
2. What are the reasons for these differences?
3. Which way is the correct way to solve the problem? Which way is better? Is it an either/or situation?
4. Can this become a win-win situation?

Handout 5: Chitchat

The following conversation takes place between Bill Burns and Tsutomu "Tom" Yoshida, coworkers in a manufacturing plant in the United States.

Bill: Hi there Tom! How ya' doin'? (Looking directly at Tom and smiling throughout the conversation.)

Tom: Hi Bill. Fine, thank you. (Looking down at the floor and smiling.)

Bill: Pretty bad weather today, isn't it? (Looking at Tom.)

Tom: Yes it is. (Looking at the other side of the room.)

Bill: How was your weekend?

Tom: How...? (Glancing at Bill quickly.)

Bill: Yeah, did ya' do anything on the weekend?

Tom: Oh, on Saturday, I took my wife shopping. On Sunday, we went to the Cedar River Park. (Looking down, then quickly at Bill.)

Bill: Cedar River Park? That's a great place. Me and some friends went camping there a couple of times. Great fishing.

Tom: Yes. It was a nice place. (Thinking, "What should I say? Why is he asking so many questions...?")

SILENCE

Bill: (Thinking, "Maybe he doesn't want to talk. Why is he only giving me these short answers. I'll give it another try....")

Uh, well, uh, I hear your wife is expecting. When is the big day?

Tom: Big day?

Bill: Yeah, when is the baby due?

Tom: Oh, I think in June. (Looking down at the floor, no facial expression.)

Bill: I bet you're excited. Is this your first?

Tom: First? (Glancing at Bill.)

Bill: Yeah, first kid.

Tom: Yes, it is. (Thinking, "I feel uncomfortable talking about my wife. Why do Americans ask so many questions—I can't think of any answer....")

SILENCE

Bill: (Thinking, "It doesn't sound like he cares too much about his family. I sure would be excited if it were my first kid.")

Well, I guess there is a lot to learn. Are you hoping for a boy or a girl?

Tom: Uh, I don't know.

Bill:	(Thinking, "Come on, ask me something!")
	I bet your wife must get lonely, ya' know, homesick?
Tom:	Yes, she sometimes get lonely.
	SILENCE
Bill:	(Thinking, "This is hopeless. I can't get anything out of this guy.")
	Well, I better get back to work. Take it easy, Tom.
Tom:	(Thinking, "Great, I can finally relax. English is too difficult for me. Why do Americans talk so much?")
	Okay. See you.

Discussion Questions

1. What are some of the communication problems between Bill and Tom?
2. How does each person perceive the other's behavior?
3. Can you explain some of the cultural and linguistic reasons behind the mis-communication?
4. How can this situation be improved?

Handout 6: The "Right Man" for the Job

The following situation took place at a Japanese subsidiary in the United States. The company was newly constructed and workers were being interviewed for various positions in the plant. The type of manufacturing was dirty, hot, and dangerous, as it involved production of steel powder from molten metals. Two Japanese managers were conducting the interviews based on the following criteria:

Position
Production Dept., forklift operator.

Duties
Operate forklift for transporting 400+ kilo (880+ lb.) drums of material to the warehouse, some physical lifting or moving of 30 kilo (66 lb.) crates.

Requirements
Forklift Operator's License, previous experience of two or more years, good work record by previous employers, ability to pass company physical exam, intention to stay on with the company for two or more years.

Candidate
Wilma Peters (female).

Physical Description (for case-study purposes)
Height: 164 cm. (5 ft. 5 in.); Weight: 80 kgs. (176 lbs.); Status: single; Age: 37.

Qualifications
Forklift Operator's License, 1st Class (highly skilled), worked successfully for five years at paper mill (laid off for economic reasons), excellent work record, good physical condition (minor: twenty pounds overweight, but allowable for job), seeking long-term employment, likes plant work very much, is interested in Japan, is studying basic Japanese for fun.

The Interview

Mr. Sasaki: Well, Miss Peters, uh, it is "Miss," isn't it? (Thinking, "She's a big woman, but pretty.")

Wilma: Uhm, actually, I don't see what difference it makes….You don't need to know that, do you?

Mr. Sasaki: Well, we are a small company and we take great interest in our workers. We don't want to have your personal details, but we heard that you know one of our maintenance staff—uh, Larry Swensen?

Wilma: Uhm, yeah, I know him fairly well. He was the one who told me about the job opening here.

Mr. Sasaki:	I see. I hear that you moved here together from Des Moines, Iowa. (Thinking, "I wonder why they aren't married?")
Wilma:	Uhm, did he tell you that?
Mr. Sasaki:	Well, he mentioned it to Mr. Fuji here. (Indicating his colleague sitting next to him at the interview table. Mr. Fuji continues to show no facial expression.)
Wilma:	Oh. Well, in that case, yeah. We've been seeing each other for some time. But I don't see…
Mr. Sasaki:	(Interrupting.) Ah, don't worry. It is no problem here. We see you have a very good work record. Tell me, why do you do this kind of work? (Thinking, "She should be at home taking care of children, or doing some nice part-time work….")
Wilma:	Sorry?
Mr. Sasaki:	Well, uh, you see, the plant here is very hot and dirty and…
Wilma:	(Interrupting.) To be frank with you, I've been in worse conditions— at my previous job. That doesn't bother me much. I like to keep real busy, and operating this kind of machinery is a challenge. I've always liked this kind of "hands-on" work. Something that's physical, you know.
Mr. Sasaki:	Eeeehhh? (Japanese expression showing surprise or disbelief.) Uh, well, I see you request the midnight shift.
Wilma:	Yeah. I prefer working nights. I really don't want to be on the day shift. It shouldn't be a problem…lots of people hate the graveyard shift. As for me, I get more work done. Time goes faster.
Mr. Sasaki:	But uh, I think Larry works in the day shift. He is a very fine worker. Does he know you wish to work at midnight? (Thinking, "He should not allow her to work so late.")
Wilma:	Yeah. No problem. He's a day person. I'm a night person. Why should that make a difference? (Thinking, "My personal life is none of his business.")
Mr. Sasaki:	I'm sorry. No difference, but uh, you know you will be the only woman in the plant late at night. I'm afraid it might be a problem.
Wilma:	Problem? I don't understand…. (Thinking, "Why isn't that other guy asking me anything. He just keeps staring at me….")
Mr. Sasaki:	Well, uh, you know. There is no protection for you…. Workers may get the wrong idea. (Thinking, "She will probably require one day off per month, as well….")
Wilma:	Are you serious? (Thinking, "I can't believe he said that.")
Mr. Sasaki:	Well, uh, sorry, we feel some responsibility. Perhaps it will also cause some trouble for Mr. Swensen.

Wilma:	Look, I don't think this should interfere with my qualifications and work record....
Mr. Sasaki:	Yes, yes. Don't worry. You see, we are just concerned....We will highly consider your application. Please wait for our call in a day or so.
Wilma:	Yeah, okay. (Thinking, "I don't believe it. Wait till I tell Larry about this!")

(Wilma leaves the room. Sasaki looks at his colleague and makes a sucking noise through the side of his mouth.)

Discussion Questions

1. What are some of the specific cross-cultural problems in this situation?
2. How does each side perceive the other?
3. What are some of the legal _____ personnel in the United States and in Japan? How d _____ ind norms concerning women?
4. What are the future implications of this situation? (How could it affect the Japanese company?)
5. Are the Japanese fully aware of the impact of their behavior?

Section V: Analyzing Cross-Cultural Incidents (activities 25-29)

Introduction

"Incidents" is a euphemism for "foul-ups." That is what frequently happens when people from two distinct cultures interact. Not all the time, but often enough.

Elijah Lovejoy calls these incidents "red flags" of warning that a cultural misunderstanding has occurred. The setting for his activities is in an overseas culture. He describes three types of red flags: negative red flags that involve instinctive annoyance or anger at the behavior of members of the unfamiliar culture; positive red flags, where things seem to be better than they really are; and reciprocal red flags, where members of the host culture react to you in an unexpected way—they get angry, laugh, or are surprised. These red flags signal that something has transpired that requires further analysis. Each of these three types of warnings is the subject of a separate activity.

Peggy Pusch provides a training framework for critical incidents. You can take any critical incident and put it in this format and *voilà*—you have a short, economical training unit running between 10 and 20 minutes (or you can usually stretch them out if you have time or they generate especially productive discussion). Anyone who has lived in another culture can easily generate critical incidents; a group of experienced sojourners can draft a number of them in 20 minutes. Pusch gives three examples of critical incidents that enable the trainer to use the framework right from the start.

A variation in how critical incidents can be presented is offered by James Baxter and Sheila Ramsey. In their model, "Improvising Critical Incidents," several participants are given improvisation cards containing a brief description of their role and scenario. The selected participants then perform a role play while the rest of the group serve as observers. The participants and observers are asked to describe the interaction; Baxter and Ramsey suggest many aspects to explore (e.g., nonverbal interplay, modalities such as assertiveness or deference). This activity involves all the participants in experiential learning that leads them to realize that cultural differences in behavior can have significant consequences.

25

Negative Red Flags

Elijah Lovejoy

Objective

To correct a fair number of intercultural misunderstandings by learning to use your own subjective, emotional reactions as warning signals that there may be cultural differences at work.

Participants

People who have lived abroad or who are planning to go abroad.

Materials

Handout.

Setting

Any setting that allows for both large- and small-group activity; writing surfaces are not needed.

Time

45–90 minutes.

Procedure

1. Have participants who have experience living in another country stand on one side of the room. Divide other participants into small groups of 3–4 (if there are over 30 participants, use groups of 4–5), then have the people who have lived abroad join a group that doesn't have any experienced sojourners.

2. Distribute the handout.

3. Invite each group to read the red flags (perhaps a different group member would read each red flag aloud for the group), then discuss in their small groups whether anything like that ever happened to them when they were observing or interacting with people from another racial/ethnic/national group. At the end of the discussion, each group selects one of the best personal examples to share with the other participants.

4. Reassemble participants into one large group. Each small-group spokesperson relates his or her chosen example of how one of the members of the group experienced a negative red flag.

5. Facilitator leads discussion on how to deal with negative red flags. Points that can be made include:

   o *Red flags are prompts to get us thinking about cultural differences, about the possible differences in the meaning of similar behaviors in the home and host cultures.* You can use your own reactions and those of others as warning signals—red flags—to prompt the beginning of a cultural analysis.

   o *Sometimes you can figure things out alone, but at other times it is helpful to ask people from the other culture to help you understand the meaning of the red flag.* People from the host culture who have lived in your culture as well often make especially good resources. They will have encountered some of the same differences that the visitor is seeing and will be able to aid the visitor in understanding the point of view of the local people.

   o *Talking with other foreigners can help, too.* It might be a good idea to start or join a group of people from various cultures who meet to discuss their cross-cultural experiences. Often people from various cultures will have quite different perceptions of the same host culture. By comparing these perspectives, one can gain an improved understanding of the situations that have been detected by using the red flags. For example, English people living in France get upset because the French "don't know how to stand in line." This is a major source of annoyance to the English. It helps to enlarge their perspective if they talk with Italians living in France. Some Italians are vociferous in their objections to the propensity of the French to stand in lines: "They spend their life in lines, always queuing! What a bore! It's so dead! I prefer the way we handle such situations in Italy. There, things are more sporting, and you can get things done more quickly!"

   o *Look for parallels between the home and host cultures when a red flag occurs.* For example, many Americans get upset when traveling in Mexico because a small bribe, *la mordida,* is sometimes required to get things done. The Americans are likely to feel morally superior to their hosts. It would help in this situation for the Americans to reflect on the various mechanisms that exist in the United States to help get things done more efficiently, including tipping. Bribes are not common in the United States, but many Americans think nothing of calling on a friend who works in an office when they need something done by that office, of using a connection to find employment, or of having a friend help in buying at a lower price. Such tactics for obtaining special privileges are common in the United States (and Mexico), and they may serve a purpose somewhat similar to that played by la mordida in other countries. The person who has looked for parallels in the two countries may make progress in understanding both.

○ *If we overlook cultural differences and interpret another individual's behavior according to our own cultural rules, serious errors are likely to occur sooner or later.* To some extent, such errors are bound to happen; no one can know every subtle detail of a new culture when he or she first arrives, regardless of how much investigating was done beforehand. Careful use of our own subjective reactions as warning signals, or red flags, can help to reduce more rapidly the amount of miscommunication and misunderstanding between ourselves and our hosts.

Further Reading/Reference

Kohls, L. Robert. *Survival Kit for Overseas Living.* 3d ed. Yarmouth, ME: Intercultural Press, 1996.

This activity and the next two are based on an essay by Elijah Lovejoy (recently retired from the Department of Psychology, University of California at Santa Barbara) and were adapted by the editor to fit the current book's format. Lovejoy's essay appears as Resource 16 in Cornelius Grove, *Orientation Handbook for Youth Exchange Programs.* Yarmouth, ME: Intercultural Press (1989): 149–56.

Handout: Negative Red Flags

The red flags that occur most often are those that involve an instinctive negative evaluation of the behavior of the members of the unfamiliar culture. Four of the most common negative red flags are discussed below, and many others are listed at the end of this section.

Negative Red Flag 1: "They Are Rude!"

A visitor to the United States is talking with some Americans, and one of the Americans takes a pack of cigarettes out of his pocket and lights one without any thought. This event, which can be totally insignificant in the United States, is felt like a slap in the face by many foreign visitors with whom I have spoken. According to the implicit rules of their homelands, it is unthinkable for a person to light a cigarette without first offering cigarettes to the others in the group. "Smoking without offering" can only be interpreted as an act of deliberate rudeness or hostility.

Certain questions may be interpreted as rude: A Moroccan living in France may be shocked when French associates inquire about his wife. Such questions are a banal form of chitchat in France but may indicate to the Moroccan an improper interest in a private matter. An Ethiopian girl visiting in the United States went to a swimming pool one day with friends. She was shocked and upset when someone asked her, "How do you stay so thin?" In the United States, this is not really a request for information, but a compliment on the fashionable state of a person's body. But plumpness is desirable for Ethiopian women, so the question had an altogether unintended impact. She perceived the questioner as being rude because the question would have been rude in her homeland.

If the visitor has the ability to realize that two different meaning rules are involved, it can help to reduce the level of adrenaline. I doubt if one can avoid the initial, almost instantaneous reaction, "How rude!" But that reaction, rather than being a final judgment, can serve to initiate a careful process of reflection. It can be the starting point for an intercultural investigation. One should talk to culturally different people to find out whether the perceived rude behavior is acceptable back in their home country or whether it is just as rude there as in one's own country.

To think "They are treating me rudely!" will tend to drive the visitor away from further contact with local people. But to think "they do things here that we would find rude back home" leaves one's mind open to the realization that, very possibly, people in the host country are not acting in a way that they consider to be rude. This, of course, improves the chances of making continuing contact.

Negative Red Flag 2: "They Are Dirty!"

People in most cultures place a very strong emphasis on cleanliness. But misunderstandings arise because different groups have different definitions or customs about what constitutes the right sort and amount of cleanliness. When you come into contact with people who have different customs of cleanliness, you may judge them to be "dirty" or "picky" depending on whether they are less or more attentive to a particular sort of cleanliness.

L. Robert Kohls, in his excellent book *Survival Kit for Overseas Living*, mentions several areas in which Americans are often perceived as dirty. Kohls notes that when Americans bathe, they soak, wash, and rinse their bodies in the same water—though they would never wash their clothes or dishes that way. The Japanese, who use different water for each step of bathing, find the American way of bathing hard to understand, even dirty. Kohls asks also whether it is dirtier to spit and blow your nose on the street, or into a little piece of cloth that you keep in your pocket and reuse regularly.

Raymond Gorden, in his perceptive book *Living in Latin America*, reported a study of American students living in Bogotá, Colombia. The Americans mentioned that they had the impression that Colombians were dirty because they turned the hot water on only in the morning and washed dishes in the evening with cold water. It is revealing that the Colombians with whom the Americans lived also thought that the Americans were dirty because they did not bathe every day.

When one goes to a new culture, it may well happen that one gets the impression that the native people are dirty. Rather than stopping at this powerful negative observation, one should be able to use the reaction as a signal—a red flag—that one may have hit upon an area where there are cultural differences in what is considered to be proper cleanliness. It may be possible then to reflect constructively upon these differences instead of simply reacting in a negative way that will tend to separate one from those "dirty people."

Negative Red Flag 3: "They Are Hypocrites!"

Most cultures disapprove of hypocrisy. So the feeling that someone is a hypocrite can be a major barrier to intercultural communication.

I asked a group of California students who had been in France for about eight months how they felt about the French. "They're pretty nice," said one girl, "but they are all hypocrites. They kiss you on both cheeks, as if they really like you, but it doesn't mean a damn thing!" As she said this, several other students in the room nodded their heads in agreement. Their judgment "They are hypocrites" was wrong, however, because they had misinterpreted the meaning of "being kissed on both cheeks." In the United States, kissing may communicate an especially close relationship, but in the student population in France it means hello and nothing more. Few French people would consider *la bise* to be hypocritical.

The perception "They are hypocrites," while a very natural one, tends to stop all further reflection and to build a barrier between people from different cultures. The sojourner should learn to translate his or her complaint into a more subtle form: "I get the feeling that they are hypocrites. This could be because I have misunderstood something. I must try to find out."

Negative Red Flag 4: "They Are Stupid!"

Cultures differ in what they consider to be intelligent or stupid. The result is that visitors often find the people of their host countries deficient in this regard. In *Students as Links between Cultures*, Ingrid Eide reported a study in 1970 of students from Egypt, Iran, and India who were at school in the United States, the United Kingdom, and West Germany. She asked the sojourners to make checks on a long list of personal traits: those that applied to the nationals of their host countries and those traits that applied to their own homelands. The results were striking: 76 percent of the Egyptian students, for example, said that the trait "intelligent" applied to Egyptians, but only 28 percent said that the people in their host country were intelligent. A similar result was obtained for the students from Iran and India. Knowing that this is a common pattern may help us to start an analysis.

People from Japan staying in France are surprised to find that in many stores a transaction involves standing in line once to get a product, then again to pay the cashier. Being unused to such a system, they may react with a quick, "They are stupid!" Like other negative reactions, this one often terminates reflection. But it can help to use this reaction as a signal to try to figure out why things are arranged this way. I believe that the system in France can be traced to a basic security problem. If only the owner handles cash, then there is no chance that hired employees will act dishonestly or make costly errors. It may well be that internalized controls are quite sufficient to keep clerks honest in Japan while other forms of control may be needed in other countries.

The reaction "They are stupid" is often accompanied by very strong emotions and a sense of personal outrage. For example, the sojourner often discovers that the host nationals are ignorant or ill-informed about the sojourner's homeland. People from all parts of the world who come to the United States get upset because Americans in general seem rather uninterested in what goes on outside their own country. Another example is that Swedes who live in France discover that when they go to a movie they find an usher, or *ouvreuse*, waiting to show them to their seats and that she expects a tip for the service. This small custom triggers strong emotional reactions: "What a stupid system! I can find my own seat!" The French people, of course, give the custom little or no thought. The tip is part of the cost of going to a film. The service may seem pointless, but perhaps it's a way of fighting unemployment.

The feeling "They are stupid" may stem from basic differences in the way people think and the way they convey ideas. At one seminar involving Japanese and U.S. businessmen, an American asked a Japanese what was most difficult for him in the United States. The Japanese replied, "The most difficult part of my life here is to understand Americans. They are so irrational and illogical."

It is troubling to find out that people from another culture find one stupid or irrational. But knowing this may help one to keep things in perspective when he or she gets the impression that people in other cultures are irrational, or that they do not think clearly. The "they are stupid" reaction can serve as a red flag, a signal to think, "Something's going on here that seems stupid to me. I wonder if it seems stupid to them?"

Twenty-four Additional Negative Red Flags

There are many negative reactions that the sojourner can use to signal "Start thinking about possible differences between the two cultures." Reading through the following negative red flags may help the reader to think about other examples of the application of inappropriate meaning rules to an event in an unfamiliar culture.

"I can't accept…"

"They are cold!"

"They are dishonest!"

"I hate the [nationality]!"

"It's incredible!"

"They are insulting!"

"They are patronizing!"

"It's ridiculous!"

"It's so expensive!"

"They are uncultured!"

"They are untrustworthy!"

"Why don't they do it our way?"

"They are like children!"

"It's disgusting!"

"It makes me furious!"

"They are hostile!"

"They are inscrutable!"

"They don't respect me!"

"They are primitive!"

"It's shocking!"

"It's uncomfortable!"

"They are unfriendly!"

"They are unpredictable!"

"They are years behind us!"

26

Positive Red Flags

Elijah Lovejoy

Objective

To broaden the perspective introduced in Activity 25, "Negative Red Flags," to include situations where things appear to be better or more pleasant than they actually are, again because of a difference in cultural meaning. (Positive red flags can be more hazardous than negative red flags because an inappropriate expectation of something pleasant is quite likely to lead to disappointment [events 1 and 2], or an unexpectedly "happy" event can lead to a feeling of guilt [event 3]).

Participants

People who have lived abroad or who plan to live in another culture. Maximum of 30.

Materials

Handout.

Setting

No special requirements.

Time

40 minutes (about 8 minutes for debriefing each of the three events, plus about 15 minutes to debrief all three events).

Procedure

1. Do *not* tell the participants the name of this activity, since part of it consists in having them associate—on their own—its three "positive" situations with those negative red flags described in Activity 25.
2. Distribute handout and give the participants a minute or so to read the first event (Yuri's experience in the United States).

3. Lead discussion of this event. Questions to ask may include:
   o What is Yuri's view of Americans?
   o What does he base this view on?
   o Has he appraised this accurately?
   o Will the friendly Americans Yuri meets remember some weeks later their invitations for him to drop by? How durable are friendships with strangers in the United States?
   o Do you think signs of friendship are the same almost everywhere?
   o To what do friendships obligate you in the United States? Are the obligations of friendship the same in other cultures?

4. Give participants a minute to read the second event (the Parisian dinner "date"). Lead discussion of this event. Questions to ask in the debriefing may include:
   o What happened?
   o Did either the Dutch woman or the French man have unrealistic expectations? Why?
   o Would this kind of misunderstanding happen in other countries as well?
   o Under what conditions can men and women develop close friendships that do not involve sexual intimacy?

5. Give participants a minute to read the third event (the American botanist in Mexico). Lead discussion of this event. Questions to ask may include:
   o What happened?
   o Should the American accept the gift?
   o If no, how could he have gotten out of the situation without hurting the gardener's feelings?
   o If yes, should the American do anything in return?
   o If the American gives some gift in return, should it involve a degree of sacrifice similar to that of the Mexican's? Or should it just cost the same? How do you decide on the value of a gift? What are the obligations of gift giving? Do these differ across cultures?

6. Now lead participants to find the similarities among the three events and their implications for sojourners in another culture. Questions may include:
   o What do these three events have in common? (Possible answer: Some sort of cultural misunderstanding.)
   o The misunderstandings all share a common dynamic. What is it? (Possible answer: One party projected his sense of the rules of friendship onto another cultural setting.)
   o Was there a sign that a misunderstanding may have lurked ahead? (Possible answer: In the first two events, the unexpected pleasure Yuri and the Frenchman experienced may have been a clue that disappointment was around the corner.)

- ○ Can you think of another activity we did where there were signs that all was not well? (Possible answer: In the "Negative Red Flags" activity.)
- ○ What do you think about the value of both negative and positive red flags? (Possible answer: Both can be useful signs of a cultural misunderstanding.)

Handout

Event 1

Yuri, an exchange student from Russia, was gratified by the warm reception he got upon his arrival in the United States. He was greeted by broad smiles and frequently was invited to homes for meals. Several times he was invited to stay in American homes. At cultural events, people would say to Yuri, "You must drop by and see us sometime."

Yuri called home and enthusiastically told his family that "Americans are so friendly! We are going to be close friends and see a lot of each other."

Event 2

A Dutch woman living in Paris enjoyed talking with a French friend and invited him to her apartment for dinner one evening. The meaning she intended to convey was "we are going to eat dinner together and have a nice conversation" and nothing more. But her friend interpreted the gesture as implying an invitation for sexual intimacy. He discovered the miscommunication in the middle of dinner. At this point the French man stood up and said, "You don't think I'm going to cross Paris just to have dinner, do you?" and stormed out the door.

Event 3

An American botanist, visiting a Mexican friend in Guadalajara, had the opportunity to go to the home of his friend's gardener to see some seedlings the gardener was growing. Invited to come inside the home, a very small adobe house with an earthen floor, the American was struck by the gardener's poverty. An unfinished pine table and a couple of wobbly chairs were all the furnishings in view. He then noticed a beautiful, large serape on one wall. "What a beautiful serape," exclaimed the American. "Wonderful colors!" At this, the gardener insisted that the American take the serape as a gift. The American was aware that it was a form of politeness in Mexico for a person to tell someone who admired something of his or hers that the object was theirs (*Es suyo* or *Está a la orden*). But what was happening in the gardener's home was not a polite perfunctory gesture; the man insisted the American take the serape. In fact, he even removed it from the wall and pressed it into the American's hands. The American, realizing that the weaving was the only thing of value in the whole household, did not know what to do. Later, telling this story back in the United States, he would shake his head and say, "Mexicans are so generous!" This generosity should have been promptly—and generously—reciprocated. (The American should have really tried to avoid accepting the serape. Perhaps saying something on the order of "Thank you very much, but it looks so beautiful on your wall that that is how I want to remember it...."") In many cultures, such as in Japan, it is the custom to give gifts, but it is expected that the giver will return the favor.

27

Reciprocal Red Flags
Elijah Lovejoy

Objective
To review the previous negative and positive red flags (see previous two activities) and to alert participants to another valuable form of intercultural feedback: when people from another culture react in unexpected ways.

Participants
People who have lived abroad or who plan to live abroad.

Materials
Handout.

Setting
No special requirements.

Time
10–20 minutes.

Procedure
1. Facilitator reviews the findings of the previous two activities on red flags and draws out the points that:
   - your emotional reactions—either negative or positive—to behavior of people from other cultures is a valuable clue to possible misunderstandings caused by cultural differences;
   - some of the previous negative red flags were: "They are rude!" "They are dirty!" "They are hypocrites!" "They are stupid!"
   - some of the previous positive red flags were: "They are so friendly!" "We are going to be intimate friends!" "They are so generous!"

2. Facilitator asks the participants whether they can think of another source of feedback as they interact with people from another culture to alert them to a cultural difference that might have raised its mischievous head and then draws out at least these three red flags:
   ○ "They are angry with me!"
   ○ "They are surprised at my behavior!"
   ○ "They are laughing at me!"
3. Distribute handout. Give participants 2-3minutes to read it.
4. Facilitator invites participants to share their personal experiences of unexpectedly eliciting anger, surprise, or laughter because of cultural differences in perceiving and interpreting some action.

Handout: Reciprocal Red Flags

Reciprocal Red Flag 1: "They Are Angry with Me!"

A study abroad program director in England regularly asks her students, "Has anybody become angry with you this week?" The students sometimes recall cases in which someone did get angry with them and then begin a cultural analysis to attempt to understand what they had done that was inappropriate in England. A discussion of these incidents with the program director often leads to a better understanding of the students' native culture as well as of English culture.

A French woman working in California tells of the following incident. She was driving on a large highway when she saw a police car behind her with a bright red light on. She wondered what was happening but kept on driving. In France the police always drive beside a car and signal the driver if they want the car to stop. Since the policeman behind her did not do this, she kept driving. Only when the police car turned on its siren did she pull over and stop. She was puzzled when the police officer was angry with her. Thinking back on the incident later, however, she could see that her behavior, which made perfectly good sense according to French rules, was not appropriate from the point of view of a California policeman.

When a host national gets angry, it is a good idea to start thinking. Many of us stop thinking and react emotionally when someone becomes angry with us. But even if one has not learned to inhibit his or her emotional reactions, these reactions can still be used as signals to begin a systematic cultural analysis in order to determine what went wrong.

Reciprocal Red Flag 2: "They Are Surprised at My Behavior!"

When living in France, I opened a checking account in a French bank. I casually asked the bank manager, "What do you do if I write a check for which there is no money in the bank?" The banker looked very surprised, paused for about fifteen seconds, cleared his throat, and said in a severe tone of voice, "I certainly hope that will never happen!" I tried to reassure him that I didn't intend to let it happen and let the subject drop. Some time later I asked some French friends why this was such a surprise to the banker. I learned that "bouncing a check" is much more serious in France than in the United States. To do so is a criminal offense. In this situation, I was able to use the reciprocal red flag "They are surprised" as a cue to start an analysis; consequently, the experience was educational.

Reciprocal Red Flag 3: "They Are Laughing at Me!"

It is likely that at some point a sojourner in a new culture will behave in what seems a perfectly normal way, only to find that the natives burst out laughing. There are two common reactions to this experience: One may feel humiliated and hurt, or one may be able to laugh with the others, even before completely understanding the humor of the situation. Later, the visitor may be able to find out what made his or her hosts laugh. This is such a common cross-cultural experience you should be able to draw a wealth of examples from any participant who has spent any time abroad.

How a person reacts to such an experience depends on many factors. But if the visitor can manage to laugh with the hosts and to explain the perfectly natural fact that certain things are unfamiliar, the experience can be a positive one. Later, the visitor may be able to put him- or herself in the hosts' shoes and imagine what the situation must have looked like from their point of view.

Framework for Using Critical Incidents

Margaret D. Pusch

Objective

To uncover and analyze the cultural components of an incident in which misunderstanding or conflict has occurred.

Participants

Any number.

Materials

Copies of handout for each participant.

Setting

No special requirements, but it is best if people can sit in a circle or around a table.

Time

Variable.

Procedure

1. Copies of *all* the incidents you plan to discuss are distributed to the participants. It is useful to have a set of 3 to 12 from which to choose; the handout at the end of this activity lists 3.
2. Divide the participants into small groups and ask each group to discuss one incident (assigned by the instructor), answering the following questions:
   a. What is the problem?
   b. How can it be resolved?
3. Have small groups reconvene after about 20 minutes of discussion (or whenever the instructor notices people have finished) and report on the results of their discussion.

4. The instructor assists participants in identifying the cross-cultural issues involved and uses those issues to illustrate the basic concepts and processes of intercultural communication and cross-cultural relations.

This activity is an adaptation of one appearing in *Multicultural Education: A Cross-Cultural Training Approach*, edited by Margaret D. Pusch. Yarmouth, ME: Intercultural Press (1979): 195–97.

Handout: Sample Critical Incidents

1. Lu Chen Chang applied for a scholarship to assist her with her educational expenses. In an interview with the scholarship committee she explained that her father had recently suffered a stroke and was no longer able to assist her financially. Since her grades were good, the interviewing committee sought primarily to determine the extent of her financial need. Lu Chen indicated to the committee that she had taken a part-time job but was unwilling to say anything about the job. When questioned about her part-time work she answered only, "I'd rather not say."

   Afterwards, during the committee review of her application, several members remarked that it was strange that Lu Chen refused to discuss her part-time job. One member remarked that perhaps she was afraid to disclose her wage earnings because they might disqualify her for the scholarship. Another member hinted that she might be involved in some illegal or immoral activity.

2. María González, a Puerto Rican student who had been getting excellent grades during the first half of her sophomore year, began to have trouble. When her adviser asked about it, she said she was upset at having broken up with her boyfriend, Bob Williams. The adviser tried to help her gain perspective, but it didn't seem to do any good.

   María said the problem was that she couldn't understand what had happened. They had already talked of marriage. She had gone with him to visit his home in Ohio and had liked his mother and father. They had been kind and friendly. In New York her family took to Bob at once and welcomed him fully.

   After that he grew cool toward her and finally stopped seeing her. The only reason he would give was that he didn't want to be smothered.

3. Raphael García and Alfredo Pérez started out as close friends in college. They had grown up together in the Chicano section of the city, gone to high school together, worked for Chicano civil rights, and gone on to the city's major university.

   Once in college, however, they began to grow apart. Raphael found the stimulus of an academic environment exciting and turned his attention avidly to his books. He also made new friends among Anglos as well as Chicanos. At about the same time his family moved to another city and he took up residence in a dorm. Alfredo, on the other hand, continued to be more committed to his community, his old friends, and the cause.

   When they got to their senior year, Raphael was elected student body president and Alfredo led a sit-in protesting the anti-Chicano statements of one of the Anglo vice presidents of the university.

   Each opposed the action of the other and their friendship ended in a bitter quarrel, with Raphael claiming he could do more for Chicanos within the system and Alfredo arguing that the only way to help Chicanos was in opposition to the system.

Improvising Critical Incidents

James Baxter and Sheila Ramsey

Introduction

The following discussion, with its suggested activity, brings together two methodologies relevant to intercultural work: the critical incident and improvisation. In addition, the theoretical frame of interaction analysis supports the discussion and analysis of this activity with participants.

The activity is especially interesting and relevant for the intercultural context because of the "real-time" nature of the interaction that arises through using a nonscripted improvisational approach. A critical incident, often used to promote cognitive understanding, can become the source of affective and behavioral learning.

In our experience, participants become especially motivated by the immediately applicable creative possibilities for interacting from a more informed base of awareness than becomes apparent in this type of short yet engaging learning activity.

Theoretical Background

Critical-Incident Analysis

In the early 1950s, American researchers developed a structured method of observing and recording human behavior, which was soon named the "critical-incident technique." An incident was defined as a segment of observed human behavior which by itself permitted inferences to be made about the persons involved in the behavior. An incident was deemed *critical* if the intent of the observed acts was clear and the consequences reasonably predicted (Flanagan 1954).

In the field of intercultural communication, the critical incident evolved into a standard training methodology. Other terms sometimes used to describe this training methodology are "cultural encounter" and "culture bump" (Archer 1986). As the term is now generally understood, a critical incident describes an incident of intercultural misunderstanding. The written description of the incident is concise and narrowly focused on a small set of identifiable cultural factors.

Although volumes of prepared critical incidents exist, trainers can build their own "cultural encounter" files; the best content for incidents comes from actual experience. Trainers can draw on personal experience or observation, reports from others, books and articles (providing other analyzed and unanalyzed cases), and nonprint materials such as videotapes. One simple way to maintain a cultural encounter archive is by recording incidents on separate index cards or in separate computer files so that each incident can be easily located and developed as a training exercise. It is always helpful to record observed cultural encounters as soon as possible after they occur, so as to recall accurately all relevant details of the situation.

Several categories of detail and information are vital to record about such encounters:

o Participants' nationality or cultural background, age, and sex
o Role relationships
o Goal of the communication or activity
o Nonverbal aspects of the interaction
o What was said and done
o Reactions of participants and of observers/bystanders
o Environment (e.g., time of day, physical conditions, location)

Critical-incident analysis presents learners with a microcosm of intercultural interaction. The analysis of a real-life intercultural interaction can lead participants from an understanding of specific behaviors to a recognition of underlying cultural generalizations. Through directed questioning, learners *identify cultural factors, trace causes of misunderstanding,* and *recognize the consequences of misunderstanding.* Most important, learners become aware of the interactional dynamics of cultural encounter.

Interaction Analysis

Throughout any workshop, the trainer must keep the focus on intercultural interaction. Intercultural effectiveness is not the mathematical addition of "own culture" plus "other culture." A complex interactional process is generated when individuals of different cultural backgrounds are brought together in one context. There is also the additional dynamic of certain individuals having to use the first language of the other individuals in the context. Thus, in introducing culture-specific information and in leading and debriefing workshop exercises, the trainer must constantly point out aspects of the process of intercultural interaction.

Underlying a cultural-awareness workshop, then, will be an approach which can be referred to as *interaction analysis* (Baxter 1983; Erickson 1975; Gumperz 1977 and 1978; Gumperz, Jupp, and Roberts 1979; Ramsey 1983). Basic to intercultural competence is the ability to learn from instances of intercultural miscommunication. But the ability to reflect upon an act of communication depends upon a knowledge of the types of variables involved in that act. To a person without such knowledge, an act of communication can appear to be a vast uncharted terrain.

Thus, one component of cultural awareness is the ability to *map communication*. An interactional approach can assist learners in developing the ability to create a map of interactions.

This analytic approach, as one vital component of working with critical incidents, gives a cognitive understanding of culture's influence on behavior and of the cultural consequences of an individual's behavior. It is also important to involve participants in affective and behavioral learning. As this becomes the case, it is possible to change the form within which a critical incident is explored. That is, the same theme that was cognitively analyzed can become the basis for improvisation.

Improvisation

Situations can be improvised by workshop participants prior to analysis. The key to improvisation is that *participants do not know ahead of time the details of their interaction.* It is not scripted. An element of conflict or potential miscommunication can give direction to the improvisation. Improvisation cards are given to the participants in the exercise to describe key aspects of the situation. It is important that the participants not see one another's cards, for it is the difference in information given which generates the improvisation. (For a brief discussion of improvisation see Via 1976, 24-28).

The following improvisation activity uses the technique of *role reversal*—having someone take on the behavior characteristics of another culture. The trainer may ask the employee, "Was this easy for you to do? Were you comfortable? How does it feel to act in a way different from the usual?" These types of questions can lead into a discussion of cultural adaptation and the difficulties involved and thus deals with the ethnocentric position of: "They're here in this country, and they just have to learn our culture."

The Improvised Activity

Objective

To demonstrate that culture influences one's response to feedback.

In the following example, based on a real encounter, the focus is on positive feedback given from a supervisor to an employee, in a work setting.[1] Depending upon the personalities and the cultural backgrounds of the participants, the outcome of the improvisation will vary.

Participants

6–20.

Materials

Improvisation cards for participants: A, B, C (provided).

Setting

No special requirements.

Time

30–40 minutes.

Procedure: Scene I

Steps:

A. Ask two persons to participate in the improvisation. Give each either improvisation card A or B.
B. Explain the general setting to the others in the workshop.
C. Ask them to act as observers.
D. The improvisation takes place.

Improvisation Card for Participant A

You are a first-line supervisor in an electronics firm. One of your hourly employees has been demonstrating particularly good performance over the last few months: good attendance, always meeting production quotas, and contributing to team rapport. You want to give positive feedback about this, letting him/her know that you see him/her as a "top performer." You find an opportunity today: You walk into the company cafeteria and see him/her sitting alone.

---

[1] The actual cultural encounter underlying this improvisation was one in which a U.S.-born supervisor gave praise to an employee from Taiwan. The employee, in response to the supervisor's "positive feedback," replied, "Oh, no, no. It is thanks to you that I am doing a good job. You choose the right things for me to do." The supervisor saw this as a lack of self-confidence, of self-esteem—a perception having significant consequences in regard to the employee's job advancement.

Improvisation Card for Participant B

You are an hourly employee at an electronics firm. You would like to move up to a lead position. You've really been trying over the last few months to improve your job performance. You'd like your supervisor to notice you. Right now, you're on coffee break and are sitting by yourself in the company cafeteria.

Leading the Discussion: Scene I

In leading a discussion of the improvisation, the following perspectives should be held in the trainer's mind:

Exactly what was the "employee's" behavior/assumption in responding to the compliment/positive feedback? What was the "supervisor's" behavior/assumption in giving such feedback?

How did each player *learn* to respond/make assumptions in this way?

Were the behavior and assumptions appropriate, given the setting?

Steps:

E. The trainer can start the discussion by asking the observers, "What did you see? What were they doing?" It generally takes a moment before the group observes that the "supervisor" was praising the "employee."

F. The trainer then alternately questions the observers, the employee, and the supervisor.

G. If the participants in the improvisation are both U.S.-born, the outcome, based upon the experience of using this incident, may be as follows:

At the beginning of the improvisation, observers comment that there is a moment of sparring. The employee explains that this is because it was unclear what the supervisor wanted, and so the employee was being careful. When the supervisor begins to praise the employee, observers note that the employee sits in a relaxed manner (often with legs crossed), maintains steady eye contact, and smiles. In response to praise, the employee says things such as "Why, thank you," "Well, I feel I have been improving my performance," "That's nice to hear." After a moment, the employee may even broach the subject of the desire to be promoted to a lead position. The observers see the employee as being self-confident and somewhat assertive. The supervisor shares this perception.

When asked, "Would you consider promoting me to a lead position?" the supervisor says "Yes." U.S.-born observers see the employee's behavior as being appropriate. Non-U.S.-born observers may not agree with this, however, and the trainer should explore their perceptions. Bringing in the notion of culture learning, the trainer asks the employee, "How did you learn to respond to praise in this way? Did someone teach you to say 'Thank you' to a compliment?" The employee may mention several sources of learning, but the answer is usually that no one formally taught him/her this behavior.

Procedure: Scene II

Steps:

H. At this point, ask another person to participate in a second improvisation. The setting is exactly the same, with the same person as "supervisor." There is a change of "employee." The new participant takes the same employee improvisation card as before but in addition is given improvisation card C.

I. The improvisation takes place as before, with workshop participants observing.

Improvisation Card for Participant C

You are an employee at the electronics firm. The situation is the same, except:

You are from Taiwan. You hold the cultural values of group harmony and recognition of hierarchy. Whenever you receive a compliment or praise, you feel that the appropriate response is to deny this, crediting the group or someone in higher status than you. You feel that explicitly accepting praise would make you stand out from your work group—something which you do not want to do.

Leading the Discussion: Scene II

Steps:

J. Lead a discussion of the second improvisation.

With a U.S.-born participant playing the role of the Taiwanese employee, the outcome tends to be as follows:

The employee sits forward in the chair, knees together, hands in the lap. There is an avoidance of eye contact (i.e., the U.S.-born participant tries to *avoid* eye contact, but is usually unable to do so throughout the improvisation). In response to praise, the employee says things such as, "Oh, no," "My group is very good," "It's because you are a good supervisor." Observers see the employee as being nervous and lacking self-confidence. The supervisor shares this perception and questions whether it would be advisable to promote this person. U.S.-born observers do not see the employee's behavior as appropriate. But a Vietnamese observer in one workshop commented, "This reminds me very much of the way Indochinese women act. I think she is being polite and respectful. From her point of view, this is appropriate."

In Conclusion

The discussion of such an improvisation as this has great potential for richness and depth. The analysis of critical incidents/cultural encounters can be guided through the use of many types of questions. For example:

o What are the cultural factors in this incident? (recognition)

o Which factor or factors can be seen as causing the misunderstanding? (analysis)

o What specifically could be done to resolve this misunderstanding? (resolution)

o Given their cultural differences, what significant difficulties might arise in the future between the people involved in this incident? (anticipation) (Renwick n.d., 25)

- What culture-specific information would help the individuals in this incident avoid future misunderstanding of the sort described?
- What is the problem? What are the possible consequences of this problem?
- What skills do the individuals in the incident now have which could be used to resolve the difficulty? What new skills do they need? What are the benefits of such skills? (Gormley, McCaffery, and Edwards 1981)

To summarize, this improvisation involves workshop participants in direct experiential learning. It takes a specific area of organizational culture—evaluation and norms of feedback—and demonstrates that cultural differences in behavior can have significant consequences. It enables the trainer to deal with notions such as *culture learning, perception, nonverbal behavior,* and *analysis of intercultural interaction.*

Further Reading/References

Archer, Carol. "Culture Bump and Beyond." In *Culture Bound,* edited by Joyce Merrill Valdes. Cambridge, England, and New York: Cambridge University Press, 1986: 170-78.

Baxter, James. "English for Intercultural Communication: An Approach to Intercultural Communication Training." In *Handbook of Intercultural Training, vol. II: Context and Method of Training,* edited by Dan Landis and Richard W. Brislin. New York: Pergamon, 1983.

Erickson, F. "Gatekeeping and the Melting Pot: Interaction in Counseling Encounters." *Harvard Educational Review* 45, no. 1 (1975): 44-70.

Flanagan, J. C. "The Critical Incident Technique." *Psychological Bulletin* 51, no. 4 (1954): 327-58.

Gormley, Wilma J., James A. McCaffery, and Dan Edwards. *Peace Corps: New Strategies and Designs for Cross-cultural Training.* Workshop given at the 7th annual SIETAR conference, Vancouver: British Columbia, March 1981.

Gumperz, John J. "Sociocultural Knowledge in Conversational Inference." *Georgetown University Roundtable on Languages and Linguistics.* Georgetown University, 1977: 191-211.

————. "The Conversational Analysis of Interethnic Communication." In *Interethnic Communication,* edited by E. L. Ross. Athens, GA: University of Georgia Press, 1978.

Gumperz, John J., T. Jupp, and C. Roberts. *Crosstalk: A Study of Cross-Cultural Communication.* Background material and notes to accompany the B.B.C. film. Southall, Middlesex (England): National Centre for Industrial Language Training, 1979.

Ramsey, Sheila. "Interaction Analysis," in *Take Two: English for Intercultural Communication,* James Baxter (project director), Cliff Clarke, Deena Levine, Sheila Ramsey, and K. M. Young. Videotape and training manual. Palo Alto, CA: CATESOL and Intercultural Relations Institute, 1983.

Renwick, George. *Evaluation Handbook for Cross-Cultural Training and Multicultural Education.* Chicago: Intercultural Press, n.d. (Also available in *Multicultural Education: A Cross-Cultural Training Approach,* edited by Margaret D. Pusch. Yarmouth, ME: Intercultural Press, 1979.)

Via, R. A. *English in Three Acts.* Honolulu, HI: University Press of Hawaii, 1976.

This activity is an adapted version of one originally appearing in James Baxter and Sheila Ramsey, *Training for Cross-Cultural Communication Trainers, California Cultural Awareness Resource Guide,* edited by David Hemphill, Chinatown Resources Development Center, 1982.

Section VI: Returning Home (activities 30-32)

Introduction

The point of one of Thomas Wolfe's novels is: *You can't go home again.* Things change in your absence; the longer you are away, the more they change. This happens with your home country as well as with your family home. The passage of time affects many things, as Rip Van Winkle discovered upon waking from his deep slumber. It affects your own attitudes and behaviors as well as those of your friends and compatriots. You may be regarded as a rare bird once you return home from journeys abroad. You may *be* a rare bird!

This section contains three important activities.

In the hustle and bustle of getting ready to leave after a lengthy sojourn abroad, it is common to forget a very important task—saying goodbye to friends and acquaintances. This ritual is important for two reasons. First, it avoids hurting people's feelings (and perhaps disposing them to take less interest in the next foreigner who visits). Second, it strengthens bonds that may well last a lifetime. Judith M. Blohm provides a valuable activity to make saying goodbye a little easier.

The second, developed by Cornelius Grove, is aimed at "minimizing the effects of the *reverse culture shock* often experienced by sojourners upon their return home." The need to do this is often overlooked. Yet it is common for returning sojourners to miss acutely their adopted country and to feel somewhat out of place back in their home country. Grove provides four well-chosen and typical reentry problems faced by our dauntless traveler. Participants are divided into small groups and each is given one of the four problems; the group is asked to make one or two practical suggestions for dealing with the problem, and these are reported back to the large group.

While tourists often report that travel abroad makes them "appreciate my own country more," during a lengthy sojourn it is common for one's attitudes toward one's country of origin to become more negative. J. Daniel Hess provides an activity that allows participants to air their feelings toward an American sojourner whose view of the United States appears quite negative. This activity can be used with people who have already spent some time abroad, or as a vehicle for preparing people who plan a lengthy sojourn to recognize a commonplace dynamic of second-culture adjustment.

30

Saying Goodbye

Judith M. Blohm

Purpose

To have participants share their feelings about saying goodbye and determine some ways to say goodbye well.

Participants

Any number of people preparing to return home from overseas; especially designed for exchange students and diplomatic families, but adaptable for people of any age or status.

Time

30–45 minutes: introduction, 2 minutes; individual writing, 5 minutes; small-group sharing, 20 minutes; reporting out, 10 minutes; creative ways to say goodbye and summary, 10 minutes.

Materials

Handout, paper and pencils or pens, flip chart, tape.

Setting

Small groups.

Procedure

1. The leader introduces the session by making the following points:
   a. Perhaps one of the most difficult parts of the exchange experience lies ahead—that of saying goodbye to friends, colleagues, acquaintances, to a host family, to places and settings in which you have come to feel at home in the host country.
   b. Planning your departure and taking time to say goodbye well are going to be important. It is also very important to a smooth transition home—

ward to feel that you have not left behind "unfinished business" or left important things unsaid.

2. The leader then asks returnees to make notes on the following. (Time: about 5 minutes.)

   a. People you will miss.
   b. Places you will miss.
   c. Things you will miss.
   d. Ideas about how to say goodbye to them.

3. Now ask the returnees to form small groups of 3-5 and choose a recorder to take notes on the discussion. In the group, talk about the people, places, and things participants have listed. Everyone should be included. Tell them that in about 15 minutes you will ask them to discuss the last question, ideas about how to say goodbye.

   (As a variation, give each group a blank flip chart and several colored marking pens and ask the participants to show visually in some way the people, places, and things they will miss. These charts are then shown in step 4 when the recorder tells about the group discussion.)

   Circulate around as groups work to be sure everyone is involved.

   After 15 minutes, ask the groups to list some of their ideas on how to say goodbye to the people, places, and things they will miss. (Time: about 5 minutes.)

4. Ask groups to return to the general meeting area and have each group's recorder read the summary of the group's discussion of people, places, and things they missed. (Save their ideas on ways to say goodbye until later.)

   When all groups have reported, the leader should summarize quickly and comment on the significance of the feelings expressed: the opportunity overseas experience offers for establishing deep and meaningful relationships with people from a different culture which may be maintained despite the distance and the passage of time.

5. The leader then asks the group recorders to give some of the ideas their group had on how to say goodbye. These can be listed on a flip chart as they are mentioned. Ask for additional ideas from the group after the recorders are done.

   Then pass out copies of Handout: Creative Ways to Say Goodbye. Discuss the ideas put forth in it and compare them to those suggested by the participants.

6. The leader summarizes the entire session and concludes with some final comments on the value of finding appropriate ways to say goodbye.

This activity, based on a session from the Foreign Service Institute, was prepared for Youth for Understanding by Judith M. Blohm. It appears in Judith M. Blohm and Michael C. Mercil, *Planning and Conducting Re-Entry Orientations*. Washington, DC: Youth for Understanding (1982): 65-67.

Handout: Creative Ways to Say Goodbye

(These are oriented to exchange students and diplomatic families; others may wish to modify them or find different ways to say goodbye.)

1. Repeat a special family gathering that is your favorite, such as a picnic, a backyard barbecue, a "Christmas in June," a day at the beach or the mountains.

2. Prepare a farewell meal or party for yourself and family and/or friends which includes some special customs typical of your home country or ones you'd like to start, such as:

   a. Organizing a Latin American *despedida* (goodbye party)

   b. Giving leis

   c. Tying a string or ribbon around a friend's wrist so he or she will feel you are still close

   d. Walking around the room giving each person a farewell toast, saying something to be remembered, something funny, etc.

3. Give small gifts, including things you can't take with you, perhaps a plant, or something funny such as an unused notebook or a half-empty bottle of shampoo.

4. On the last visit with each friend, give each one two envelopes with your new address already written on them.

5. Organize a potluck party where each of your friends brings one of your favorite host country dishes.

6. Plan one last visit to your favorite places, and indulge in your favorite activities—eating pizza, going hiking, skating, or playing volleyball at the beach, or whatever.

7. (Brainstorm additional ideas.)

8. Shortly after you return home, *write or send postcards to your friends abroad!*

31

Preparing for the Return Home

Cornelius Grove

Objective

To prepare the participants for understanding and minimizing the effects of the *reverse culture shock* often experienced by sojourners upon their return home.

Participants

People who are about to return or who have just recently returned home from a lengthy sojourn in another culture. From 4-60 may participate. For those who are still abroad, this activity should be used three to six weeks prior to the time they leave for home. For people who have already returned, it should be used as soon as possible.

Materials

One copy of Handout: Four Typical Reentry Problems for each participant. The handout describes a typical reentry problem faced by people returning home following a long sojourn in another culture.

Time

1-2 hours.

Rationale

Returning home can be difficult, but relatively few people who live abroad give any thought to dealing with the difficulties. While still in the host country, sojourners can profitably reflect on their forthcoming return to their respective families and home communities. The following exercise is appropriate for student or other groups large and small.

The problems of reverse culture shock, or reentry shock, have not been given as much attention in the cross-cultural adaptation literature as those of living abroad, but they can be equally or even more severe. This stems in part from the fact that they are generally ignored—if only because the return home seems a long way off until it is upon you. But it also comes from the difficulty in thinking that returning to one's own country will be difficult. It is hard to accept that the personal changes one experiences living abroad alter the personality in ways that make the readjustment to home difficult or painful. But these changes—especially if the sojourner is relatively successful in adapting to the host culture abroad—frequently put people very much out of step with their own family and culture. Special effort is needed to help them readapt successfully.

Procedure

1. Introduce this activity by recalling that when the participants left for overseas, they probably thought about or discussed in an orientation program the topic of "expectations." It is again time to consider expectations, but now the focus is on expectations about the return to their home families and communities.

> It is easy to assume that your return to your home community and family will be more or less problem-free. After all, you are returning to your native culture, to a place where you speak the language fluently and have family members and trusted friends awaiting your arrival. But the fact is that your success in dealing with the cultural differences between your host and home communities, and the longer the time you spent in the host community, the more likely it is that reverse culture shock will cause difficulties for you.

2. Without further introduction, divide the participants at random into four small groups. If you are dealing with a large number of participants, you may wish to divide them into more groups. The small groups need not necessarily be of equal size.

3. Provide each small group with the handout and direct the group's attention to a different one of the four reentry problems. Explain that the printed statement describes an actual reverse culture shock problem that has been reported over the years by recently returned international volunteers, exchange students, business executives, missionaries, and others who have been living in a foreign culture for an extended period of time.

> Instruct the groups to spend the next fifteen to twenty minutes discussing ways in which they might deal with the assigned problem upon their return home and come up with one or two solid, practical suggestions for dealing effectively with the problem. (If the total group consists of fewer than eight people, the groups can be assigned more than one problem.)

4. Circulate among the small groups during the discussion period and act as a resource person if the need arises.

5. Reconvene the plenary session after no more than twenty minutes.

6. Ask each group to report in turn as follows:
   o Briefly state the nature of the problem (without reading from the printed statement).

    o Describe one or two possible ways of dealing effectively with the problem.

Limit each report to about five minutes. After each group has reported, open the floor for general discussion. Keep track of the time so that all groups can have their ideas discussed within the time allotted.

Note: If there have been more than four discussion groups, ask the groups that worked on the same problem to report one after the other (asking the second group not to repeat ideas reported by the first) before opening the floor to general discussion.

Trainer Tip

Emphasize that by merely engaging in this activity the participants have taken the most important single step toward neutralizing the effects of reverse culture shock. They have reduced their natural tendency to expect that their return home will be without problems. Their expectations about returning are already more congruent with what the future probably has in store. They should be less surprised by the typical problems of returning sojourners and better able to readapt smoothly to life in the home community.

Further Reading/References

Austin, Clyde N., ed. *Cross-Cultural Reentry: A Book of Readings*. Abilene, TX: Abilene Christian University Press, 1986.

Hess, J. Daniel. *The Whole World Guide to Culture Learning*. Yarmouth, ME: Intercultural Press, 1994.

Kohls, L. Robert. *Survival Kit for Overseas Living*. 3d ed. Yarmouth, ME: Intercultural Press, 1996.

This activity was published in *Orientation Handbook for Youth Exchange Programs*, Cornelius Grove. Yarmouth, ME: Intercultural Press (1989): 165-68.

Handout: Four Typical Reentry Problems

Typical Reentry Problem 1

Returnees—this is especially true of younger sojourners and students—have almost always changed and matured in numerous ways during their experience away from home. They have often grown enormously in self-assurance, in their need for independence and respect, and in their knowledge and competence regarding all sorts of things. Family members and old friends whom they will meet upon arrival back home do not realize this; they treat the returnee as though he or she were the same as on the day of departure from home. Most returnees find such treatment very hard to accept, especially if it means they are treated like children.

Typical Reentry Problem 2

Returnees—particularly those who have lived closely with host nationals for an extended period of time—find that they are sharply aware of many features of their home environment and culture that they previously never noticed, or at least never questioned. Becoming suddenly and acutely aware of so many things that were previously taken for granted is not a serious problem; the problem arises because the returnees often find themselves feeling critical of many of these things. This criticism is usually expressed to family members and old friends who in turn become annoyed with the "negative attitude" of the returnees. Even if the returnees manage to keep criticism to themselves, they are disturbed about feeling negative toward people and events in the place they call home.

Typical Reentry Problem 3

Returnees—especially those whose experiences have been particularly rich—usually come home bursting with stories, ideas, facts, and all kinds of other interesting things to tell anyone who will listen. What they find, however, is that almost everyone they talk to either will not listen for more than a few minutes, or listens politely but simply cannot comprehend the richness and vitality of the returnee's experiences. (The latter attitude often shows up in the simplistic questions asked of the returnee, such as "Do people in Guatemala know what telephones are?") Such attitudes are likely to cause the returnee to feel considerable annoyance.

Typical Reentry Problem 4

Returnees—especially if they have lived for an extended time in a culture that is much different from their home culture—bring back with them many new values and patterns of behavior. Their new ways tend to be most sharply different in relation to those of the people whom they love most dearly. This particular change occurs because in their host community they became attached to certain people (such as members of a host family) and learned how to behave toward them according to the patterns characteristic of the host culture. Upon returning home, returnees encounter people whom they also love—and begin interacting with them as they learned to interact with loved ones in the host culture. In many cases, however, the family members and old friends of the returnee are bewildered and possibly even offended by this strange behavior. They, in turn, begin to act a little strange toward the returnee…and thus the seeds of misunderstanding are sown.

My Fellow Americans

J. Daniel Hess

Objective

To illustrate that the attitudes of a sojourner change when he or she lives in another culture and that some of these changes may have repercussions upon returning home.

Participants

Any number; divide into small groups of 3-6.

Materials

Handout, paper and pencil, flip chart or chalkboard.

Setting

No special requirements.

Time

45-60 minutes.

Rationale

Sojourners seldom return home in a neutral or impartial frame of mind. Just as they carry cultural baggage with them when they leave, so they carry a different set of baggage when they return. Often, returning sojourners don't realize how consequential are the new perspectives, attitudes, opinions, and lifestyles that they have adopted during the sojourn. One experience common to many sojourners is to become highly critical of their home country's culture. When a sojourner comes to know a culture quite well and has adapted to the point of identifying with its people and integrating into their way of living, he or she may experience a new array of feelings about home and country.

In culture shock theory, the extreme form of adjusting to the second culture is called "going native" and is manifest in as thorough an imitation and adoption of the host culture's behaviors and attitudes as possible, accompanied by a denigration of the behaviors and attitudes of the home country. The opposite reaction is the "flight" syndrome, in which the home culture is seen as ideal while everything about the host culture is seen as wrong.

Procedure

1. Have the group divide into smaller groups (maximum size: 6).
2. Distribute Handout: Returnee Voices, and ask everyone to read it, then to discuss with the other members of their small group their reactions to the voices of the returnees. Have them select spokespersons to report on the group's reactions. (Allow 15 minutes for this.)
3. Invite spokespersons from the small groups to report to the whole group. Facilitator notes on the flip chart or chalkboard the points made.
4. Facilitator debriefs the large group.
   a. Was the overall reaction to the sojourners' voices positive or negative? Why?
   b. Which of the returnee voices do you most identify with? Why?
   c. Let us suppose that you live near Steven and occasionally spend an evening chatting with him. How would you respond to his criticisms?
   d. Let's say you find yourself talking to a returnee who is upset about American culture. How would you deal with that?
   e. How would you deal with an international student (not an American) who appears entirely negative about the United States?
   f. What are the advantages of maintaining a negative attitude toward your home country when you are a sojourner? Examples: In settings where anti-Americanism is rampant, this may be judicious. In adopting an anti-American stance, you may avoid some of the stereotypes the hosts have of Americans. Trying to adopt the attitudes of your hosts is a way to focus on the target culture and, therefore, learn more. Do you think this will change the hosts' view of the American?
   g. What are the weaknesses of having a negative attitude toward your home culture? Examples: You may not be entirely fair in your judgment. When you return home, you may alienate everybody. You risk slipping into a denial of your own identity; it is healthier, perhaps, to acknowledge your "Americanism" as well as your skepticism.
   h. Do you think these sojourners are just in a stage of culture shock? What may be the next stage?
   i. How do you respond to this statement by Sondra Thiederman (1991) in a book written for managers in the multicultural workplace?

      As important as it is to become conscious of your culture and aware of your own cultural point of view, this does not mean that you are expected to change that culture radically or discard it. It is all right to like and value your own ways, and, in fact, studies have shown that appreciating one's own values and way of life does not make a person any more likely to be critical of other cultures.

Managers need to be reassured that although they are being called upon to make adjustments and compromises in their interactions with culturally different workers, they are not being asked to change their essential personalities and cultural perspectives (32–33).

Do you think Thiederman's statement also applies to people who have lived for several years in another culture?

Further Reading/References

Hockman, Cynthia. *Returning Home.* Goshen, IN: Pinchpenny Press, 1989.

Thiederman, Sondra. *Bridging Cultural Barriers for Corporate Success: How to Manage the Multicultural Work Force.* New York: Lexington Books, Macmillan, 1991.

This activity was adapted by the editor from material in J. Daniel Hess's section, "Returning Home," in his book *The Whole World Guide to Culture Learning.* Yarmouth, ME: Intercultural Press (1994): 243–50.

Handout: Returnee Voices

A: To Be or Not to Be a (Proud) American

Steven went to Southeast Asia with no specific goal in mind other than to take a break from college. At the time, he considered himself a rather typical American college student, except that he was restless and wanted to see the world. He chose Jakarta, Indonesia, because a family friend lived there and knew a community center where Steven could possibly teach English.

Now, three years later, Steven lives in Bangkok, Thailand, after having resided in the Philippines for a while. He has been able to find enjoyable work as an English teacher in all three countries. Simply put, he loves Southeast Asia.

Steven is well-read, studies languages diligently, and moves in a circle of internationals that he himself labels "the politically disenchanted." "A good time" for him means sitting with friends at a street bar and chatting the evening away.

But when you listen to Steven, you hear quite a lot of snarling about the United States. It's expressed in specific grievances—the U.S. involvement in the Cambodian political realignments, Philip Morris marketing cigarettes overseas, the U.S. military presence, the foreign businessmen who patronize the infamous prostitution centers of Bangkok, the tourists who ride the elephants, the American researchers who come with their questionnaires, the American-made films that dominate the marquees, the bias of the American newsmagazines, and on and on. He has on occasion said that when he sees Americans on the streets of Bangkok, he flees, not wanting to be associated with the United States.

Steven doesn't think of himself as being a negative or cynical person, just the opposite. People like to be around him because he is good-natured and even funny. But thoughts of the United States depress him. When asked how he will readjust in the States, he says that he has no desire nor plans to return.

B: Returnees Remember

Cynthia Hockman left her American college campus to spend time overseas studying and volunteering. Upon her return she went through reentry shock, an experience that was, at first, somewhat private. But she got to thinking about it and decided to talk with other returnees. What she discovered was the material for a chapbook, later published by Pinchpenny Press, entitled *Returning Home*. The book is a type of open-microphone in which students tell of their experiences and feelings upon reentry.

We have adapted several of her statements for this activity.

Immediate and initial shock: I hated coming back. The first day—getting into Chicago—I didn't even want to be there. I got into the van and I was yelling at the driver to slow down because I thought he was driving too fast. Everything seemed to be flying by. The driver stopped at a Burger King or something and I didn't feel like going in at all.

Things have changed: I was struck by how many things had happened that I didn't know about. I was almost mad in a way—like, "Why didn't you guys tell me?"

Nobody understands: I was angry with my parents and with everybody else for not understanding why I was depressed. I just cried at the drop of a hat, and they didn't understand, but I didn't know how to explain to them. They were tired of listening to all my stories. (And I could never make the stories sound the way they really were!) It was frustrating.

I'm homesick…but I'm home: I cried and cried on the plane and on the bus…. I didn't want to come back, and so when I saw my parents, it was nice meeting them, but my mind was still back in [my host country]…. After a certain point my parents and friends didn't want to hear about it anymore, and I had absolutely no one to talk to.

Some people are so naive: Many people view China as Red China, ideology China, but when I think of China, I think of my students. It makes me mad when people say stuff like "You couldn't go many places, could you?" or "The KGB watched you, didn't they?" The KGB? This is China, not Russia.

Am I happy to be an American? Once I got to the United States, I was repulsed. The grocery store was the worst. I walked in and counted over a hundred different kinds of pop and more than that many kinds of breakfast cereal. It made me sick because it just isn't necessary. I was amazed at how much excess we have and how I had never even thought of it as excess.

Life at home bores me: I was sitting around one day after I got home. It was a cold December day. I think it was drizzling. I was so tired of lying around. My overseas travels were such a big adventure and all of a sudden I had nothing to look forward to except going back to school. I remember getting up, putting on some sweats, and just running. All of a sudden I realized that this was cathartic and I ran as fast as I could—ran and ran and ran.

Why do I feel like this? Part of reentry shock is feeling guilty about my overseas experience—feeling like mine wasn't as good as other people's—and maybe I didn't like it as much as I should have—and maybe I didn't have the best attitude all the time—and feeling like somehow I failed.

About the Authors

Thomas Baglan holds a Ph.D. from Florida State University and currently is a professor of Speech Communication at Arkansas State University.

Donald Batchelder began his career directing student exchange programs for EIL in 1959. Since then he has conducted Peace Corps training and taught cross-cultural studies at the School for International Training. A former director of Save the Children in Mozambique, he is currently writing and consulting.

James Baxter has had a varied career as an ESL instructor, linguistics teacher, and cross-cultural trainer. This has provided him with opportunities to live and work in Europe, Japan, and the United States. He is currently a human resources generalist with a U.S.-Japan joint-venture company in California.

Mary J. H. Beech, a sociologist, did her dissertation on status allocation in Calcutta and subsequently returned to India four times on research projects. She teaches her favorite course, International Perspectives on Women, and other women's studies courses, as opportunities arise.

Judith M. Blohm, a cross-cultural educator and trainer, specializes in designing materials and delivering training programs that develop skills for effective multicultural encounters.

Linda B. Catlin is a cultural anthropologist. She researches and designs management development training materials for CareerTrack in Boulder, Colorado.

Jorge Cherbosque, Ph.D., is the codirector of the University of California, Los Angeles Employee Assistance Program. He consults nationally and internationally with a variety of organizations concerned with managing diversity, cross-cultural team-building, leadership and organizational effectiveness.

Paula Chu has a doctorate in Counseling Psychology and has taught and been an administrator at both college and independent school levels. On a consulting basis, she conducts workshops and lectures on diversity, oppression, and related issues.

Donna L. Goldstein, Ed.D., has taught in the Colleges of Management, Human Resources and Education for several universities in South Florida. She is the managing director of Development Associates International, Inc., a consulting and training group based in Hollywood, Florida, specializing in organizational and personal transformation. She often speaks, writes, and conducts training on diversity issues and enhancing cross-cultural effectiveness.

Cornelius Grove, Ed.D., was director of the Center for the Study of Intercultural Learning at AFS in New York when he wrote the activity included in this volume. He is now a partner in Cornelius Grove & Associates, a consulting firm based in Brooklyn, New York, that helps Fortune 500 companies develop cross-cultural competence.

Jane Stewart Heckman, grass-roots activist and bridge builder, has a lifelong commitment to building intergenerational leadership and sustainable, economically sound communities. She founded the YWCA DuPage District in the western suburbs of Chicago in 1965 and, in 1993, was one of several cofounders of The Partnership Institute in DuPage County, designed to promote cooperation and interdependent models for the ways we live, learn, and work.

J. Daniel Hess, who holds a Ph.D from Syracuse University, has been a professor of Communication and English at Goshen College since 1964. He has directed the Goshen College Study-Service program in Costa Rica for thirteen trimesters, written nine books and been published in numerous periodicals.

Ann Hubbard is the study abroad coordinator at the University of St. Thomas in St. Paul, Minnesota.

Mary D. Imanishi holds an M.A. in Intercultural Administration from the School for International Training in Brattleboro, Vermont. She specializes in the research and design of client-based intercultural training programs for Japanese and American multinational corporations.

Donald W. Klopf (Ph.D., University of Washington), is Professor Emeritus, University of Hawaii and West Virginia University; founder and first president of World Communication Association and Communication Association of the Pacific. He is the author of forty books and 150 journal articles.

L. Robert Kohls is the author of *Survival Kit for Overseas Living* and coauthor, with John Knight, of *Developing Intercultural Awareness*. He has developed more than thirty experiential exercises for facilitating intercultural learning.

Louise Munns Kuzmarskis, poet and gardener, is presently pursuing a career in the food distribution industry.

Ruth Lambach has been a language teacher for thirty years. She is currently the Refugee Program Coordinator at Truman College where she has been since 1981.

Elijah Lovejoy is a professor of Psychology, retired from the University of California at Santa Barbara where, along with other academic responsibilities, he taught a course in intercultural psychology for twenty years and ran study abroad programs in Hong Kong, Nairobi, and Mexico City.

Michael C. Mercil has thirty years of experience in international development and intercultural training, project design, management, organizational development, and conference design and management. He has also worked with the Peace Corps and other international development organizations for twenty years. He earned his B.A. and M.A. from the University of Washington in Seattle.

George G. Otero is the founder and chairman of the board of Las Palomas de Taos, a nonprofit educational center devoted to empowering and assisting individuals and groups to actively and positively meet the challenges of our changing and diverse world. He has authored hundreds of activities on global themes. He has conducted scores of global education training programs nationwide and has worked closely with schools and organizations as they seek to include global issues in their curriculum.

Anne B. Pedersen is a licensed psychologist in New Zealand where she was a faculty member at Massey University. She was a faculty member at Harvard Summer School for five years, has been at Syracuse University since 1982, and was a senior fellow at the East-West Center, Honolulu, Hawaii. She has been chair of the Science Communication and Education Committee of the Pacific Science Association from 1979 to the present and has published in the area of cross-cultural psychology and science communication.

Margaret D. Pusch is associate director of the Intercultural Communication Institute and editor of *Multicultural Education: A Cross-Cultural Training Approach*, published by the Intercultural Press.

Sheila Ramsey, Ph.D., is an independent consultant in intercultural relations. Her background is in theater, anthropology, and communication. For the past twenty years she has worked in corporate and educational settings, designing and implementing a wide variety of programs.

Indrei Ratiu has been a cross-cultural trainer and consultant and a principal of Intercultural Management Associates in Paris, France. More recently he has been involved in the informal counseling of people suffering from drug, alcohol, and other addictions.

H. Ned Seelye specializes in the design and evaluation of training and education programs in multicultural settings. His most recent books are *Teaching Culture: Strategies for Intercultural Communication* (3d rev. ed.), *Culture Clash: Managing in a Multicultural World* (coauthored with Alan Seelye-James), and *Between Cultures: Developing New Categories of Identity in a Diverse World* (coauthored with Jacqueline Howell Wasilewski).

Gary R. Smith was Staff Associate with the Center for Teaching International Relations at the University of Denver. He is currently teaching high school world history and Advanced Placement history at West High School in Salt Lake City, Utah.

Ellen Summerfield holds a Ph.D. from the University of Connecticut and is director of International Programs and professor of German at Linfield College in Oregon. Her most recent book, *Crossing Cultures through Film,* was published by the Intercultural Press.

Sandra Tjitendero was a graduate student in the United States at the time she wrote this exercise. Her current whereabouts are unknown.

Thomas F. White holds an MBA and teaches marketing and management at Chapman University. He is completing a doctorate in public policy at the University of Colorado-Denver.

Carol Wolf holds an M.Ed. from Temple University. She is executive director of Eclipse Consultant Group and is an expert in the process of organizational change, specifically, how diversity training and change initiatives impact on the nature and structure of organizations and their leadership. A licensed psychologist, Ms. Wolf has been involved in ongoing research on the developmental processes that unfold as individuals and systems struggle with growth and change.